LAW AND MORALS

IS VOLUME

148

OF THE

Twentieth Century Encyclopedia of Catholicism

UNDER SECTION

XVI

GENERAL AND SUPPLEMENTARY VOLUMES

IT IS ALSO THE

124TH

VOLUME IN ORDER OF PUBLICATION

Edited by **HENRI DANIEL-ROPS** *of the Académie Française*

LAW AND MORALS

By NORMAN ST. JOHN-STEVAS

HAWTHORN BOOKS · PUBLISHERS · *New York*

First Edition, October, 1964

BX
1751
.A1T8
V, 148

NIHIL OBSTAT

Joannes M. T. Barton, S.T.D., L.S.S.

Censor Deputatus

IMPRIMATUR

✠ Georgius L. Craven

Episcopus Sebastopolis, Vicarius Generalis

Westmonasterii, die XXIV AUGUSTI MCMLXIV

H-9523

CONTENTS

CHAPTER I

RELIGION, LAW AND LIBERTY

The problem of the relationship of law and morals is indissolubly connected with that existing between religion and the law. Clearly if one views the State as an instrument subordinate to a particular religion, ready to carry out its behests and enforce its dictates by law, one will reach a very different conclusion about the relation between law and morality than if one regards the State as an entity with its own rights and duties, taking cognizance of the existence of the Church but quite independent of it.

In the nineteenth century the official view of the Church tended towards the first alternative and, to explain the divergence between the theoretical position and the world in which the Church actually found herself, theologians made use of a terminology, still found in some of the manuals in use in Catholic seminaries, of thesis and hypothesis. The *thesis* or the ideal relationship between Church and State is the full establishment and recognition by law of the Catholic Church as the true religion. Other Churches should have no legal status: error has no rights. Unhappily such a world is not to be found in reality and therefore the Church turns to a *hypothesis*, which is to accept the freedom of contemporary society as a temporary necessity, awaiting the day when the heretic can again be suppressed by law. The theory is summed up in the words attributed to Louis Veuillot: "When we are in the minority we demand for ourselves freedom according to your principles; when we are in the majority we refuse you this freedom according to our principles."

This view of Church–State relations is a little strange. In the first place it is odd that the world should be in a state of permanent "hypothesis" with no prospect of the "thesis" ever returning. It has about it a crude and repellent impudence which is literally breathtaking. Perhaps the best comment to be made on it was that used in connection with Monsignor Chigi, a papal nuncio in nineteenth-century Paris, that the thesis was to burn the Jews, but the hypothesis was to dine with the Rothschilds. As to the axiom "error has no rights", a bludgeon so often produced to terminate discussion on the question of religious liberty, what does it mean? Error certainly has no rights, neither has truth, since rights inhere in human persons not in intellectual abstractions.

All this muddled terminology would have met the same fate as so much other Victorian bric-à-brac and been cast out with the antimacassars and the Landseers had it not been enshrined in a number of papal utterances. One finds it in Gregory XVI's *Mirari Vos* of 1832; in the *Quanta Cura* and *Syllabus Errorum* of Pius IX; and even, suitably muted, in the Encyclicals of Leo XIII. Much ingenuity can be expended in interpreting papal Encyclicals, but I wish to confine myself to making three major points. First there is no binding *ex cathedra* statement on the subject of religious liberty, which is thus open to full discussion. Second, these papal Encyclicals are only meaningful if they are considered in the historical setting which produced them. They were framed when the Church was on the defensive against the attacks of rationalist liberalism: a Jacobin phenomenon having little in common with the nonconformist religious liberalism of England and the United States. Their condemnations of liberty are to be read as condemnations of liberty as an absolute value irrespective of the ends it is used to pursue. In the 1830's, it should be remembered, the ideas of Voltaire were at their most influential. Leo XIII had to deal with the militant anti-clericalism of the third republic. The popes were condemning not freedom in our contemporary use of the term but the subjugation of the Church to the State, and the denial to the supernatural of any part in public life. Many of the documents appeared when the Church was still bedevilled by the Roman question, a traumatic experience from which she is only now recovering. Finally, the rôle of the Church as a balancing force should be kept in mind. At a time of unbridled individualism the Encyclicals acted as a social counterweight. Today, when the threat is that of the totalitarian State, the Church emphasizes individual rights. The papal documents must thus be seen as part of an historical drama: if this is done, they offer no insuperable obstacle to an acceptable theory of religious liberty.

Of course it is possible to consider religious liberty or toleration on a purely practical basis. Persecution, it is said, doesn't work. Ideas will always prevail against the sword. But will they? Persecution has worked in the past. It eradicated Catholicism from England and kept Protestantism from Spain. The approach of Pius XII to the subject, as evidenced in his address to the assembly of Italian jurists in 1953, was also severely practical, although its timing was significant in that it came immediately after a eulogy by Cardinal Ottaviani of the Spanish confessional state. The essence of Pius XII's views is contained in the following extract:

Reality shows that error and sin are in the world in great measure. God reprobates them, but he permits them to exist. Hence the affirmation: religious and moral error must always be impeded when it is possible, because tolerance of them is in itself immoral, is not valid *absolutely and unconditionally*. Moreover, God has not given even to human authority such an absolute and universal command in matters of faith and morality. Such a command is unknown to the common convictions of mankind, to Christian conscience, to the sources of revelation and to the practice of the Church. To omit here other scriptural texts which are adduced in support of the argument, Christ in the parable of the cockle gives the following advice: let the cockle grow in the field of the world together with the good seed in view of the harvest (Cf. Matt. 13. 24–30). The duty of repressing moral and religious error cannot therefore be an ultimate norm of action. It must be subordinate to *higher and more general* norms which, in *some circumstances*, permit and even perhaps seem to indicate as the better policy toleration of error in order to promote *a greater good*.

Pius XII made clear that his principle would apply even if Catholics were in the majority, so giving a change of emphasis to official Catholic teaching on the Church–State problem, but its lack of definition of what constitute "higher and more general norms" or "the greater good" limits its usefulness. Probably it was civil peace which the pontiff had in mind. The line of argument is similar to that used by St Augustine when counselling against the suppression of prostitution in the Roman Empire: "If you do away with harlots, the world will be convulsed by lust."

The argument is also advanced that the Church is better off without State patronage. Establishment, as the Church of England has realized, has its drawbacks. The Church flourishes most where it is freest from State control, and it is not without significance that the fastest growing, most flourishing Catholic community is that found in the United States, where Church and State are rigidly separated. Finally, it is asserted that toleration is essential for the defence of Christendom against Communism. Unity in the face of this threat is essential, and the gulf between Christians of different Churches can only be bridged by mutual forbearance in order to present the maximum opposition to those who reject the value of the human person.

These points have a certain validity but they do not carry one far enough. They leave the question of religious liberty in the sphere of the contingent and the expedient. What is required is an intellectual and moral basis for a Catholic view of religious liberty. This can be provided at the political jurisprudential or theological level.

The fundamental error of those who reach conclusions that heresy must always be suppressed by the State is that they treat the problem as if it were one of deductive logic. Yet as Fr John Courtney Murray, S.J., has pointed out, this is fundamentally erroneous. The argument proceeds that men can only be saved by following the law of Christ: therefore the State must enforce the law: therefore every heretic must be exterminated or at least restrained from doing damage. This is reinforced by a specious analogy about infection. We legislate against bodily disease, how much more should we act against those diseases that kill the soul. This approach is misleading for two reasons. It ignores all questions of political theory and the delimitation of the rôles of Church and State. Secondly, it takes no account of historical fact. Yet toleration of religious liberty, which is one aspect of Church–State relations, can only be considered within these categories. The starting point of the discussion must be historical, since views on toleration do not develop from a vacuum but proceed from historical situations. The starting point of the medieval discussion was that the Catholic faith provided the unity and foundation of civil society and its preservation was thus part of the common good. Today these conditions have vanished, since civil society has come of age and stands on its own feet. The common bond today is not religion but the equal status of the citizen.

Thus the starting point of the contemporary discussion of religious liberty should be the free citizen, the human person, who creates the existential problem by his free adherence to Church or State. Now both Church and State are separate societies with their own spheres and their own rights. This was the first great political contribution of Christianity and why it was so savagely persecuted in the Roman world. It proclaimed that there was not one power but two. The Church is primarily concerned with man's spiritual welfare, the State with his material well-being. The functions overlap at many points but they are distinct. The Church cannot command an act of faith, much less can the State order one on her behalf. Equally the foundation of the State is the free consent of the individual person, through whom the authority of God is mediated. The whole discussion then shifts away from an ideal Church–State relation to the notion of the individual citizen with his juridical rights and duties.

Fr Courtney Murray follows St Thomas in treating civil society, and hence the State, as a natural institution, with its own temporal end, distinct from that of the Church. Individuals are bound by the natural law and therefore the State is bound, but the State as such is not bound by the divine positive law of which it knows nothing. Even if through its citizens it comes to know the nature of the Church and its laws, its duties are discharged by allowing the Church to pursue her mission freely. It may not usurp the mission of the Church by discharging a function it is not competent to perform, nor may it impose the definition of the Church on those of its citizens who do not freely by act of faith accept the definition.

The same line of reasoning can be pursued in establishing a moral and theological basis for toleration. The moral basis of Western society, and its chief distinguishing mark from the totalitarian societies of the East, is respect for the human person. The human person is autonomous, free and inviolable. The human person is not explicable in terms of social or religious forms, nor should he be subordinated to their purposes. He transcends them. In so far as society progresses it is principally by enabling the human person to realize himself more fully in relation to other human beings with similar aims. Discipline and conformity are the essentials of primitive societies but freedom is the hallmark of a mature and advanced society. Man finds himself in a social environment with certain political and religious doctrines, but he cannot be forced to accept them, although outward conformity may be exacted. Persecution cannot create belief. Indeed, its effect as seen in some Catholic countries has been to create a scepticism amongst the educated classes which has gravely undermined the country's religious character. Political and religious doctrine can only be adopted by assent. A particular moment of conscious assent is not necessary, although these clearly occur in individuals, but the validity of religious belief depends on a continuing day-to-day assent, which may never be specifically formulated. Once assent is withdrawn, religious belief is destroyed. Hence Cardinal Newman's remark in his letter to the Duke of Norfolk (1874): "Certainly if I am obliged to bring religion into after-dinner toasts (which indeed does not seem quite the thing), I shall drink—to the pope, if you please—still to conscience first, and to the pope afterwards."

"It is against the nature of religion", therefore, as Tertullian wrote, "to force religion; it must be accepted spontaneously and not by force; the offerings demanded, indeed, must be made willingly. That is why, if you force us to sacrifice, you give, in fact, nothing to your gods: they have no need of unwilling sacrifices." And St Augustine declared tersely: *Credere non potest homo nisi volens*. Man is essentially a free being and the essence of an act of faith is that it is a free act. "Freedom", writes Cardinal Feltin, "lies at the very heart of Christianity, which seen from without might look like a system, but thought and lived from within is a living bond between persons, a religion of the spirit. Faith is the encounter of a free gift and a free acceptance: a call on the part of God and a conscious and submissive response to God's voice." Thus the contemporary approach to religious liberty should not start from an abstract "thesis" but from the act of faith itself, in essence an act of freedom. Faith comes through the Church, but is not given by the Church but by God. A coerced act of faith, as the Church has long known, is in a real sense a blasphemy, whether the coercion is carried out by Church or State because it substitutes one or the other for the operation of the Holy Spirit. Since freedom is the essence of an act of faith, the freer it is and the more spontaneous, the more perfect it becomes. The duty of the State is, therefore, to create the conditions most favourable for the possibility of acts of faith. The Church thus requires freedom but she needs no more. There cannot of course be a right in the human person to reject God, but there is a liberty to do so. That after all is the human predicament. Man accordingly has a right against the State and the Church not to have God imposed on him against his will.

The point was put clearly by Pius XII in his Encyclical *Mystici Corporis*:

> But while we desire [said Pius XII] supplication to go up unceasingly to God from the whole mystical body, that all those who are astray may as soon as possible enter the one fold of Jesus Christ, we declare that it is absolutely necessary that this should come about by their free choice, since no man believes unless he is willing. Wherefore if any persons, not believing, are constrained to enter a church, to approach the altar and to receive sacraments, they certainly do not become true believers in Christ; because that faith without which "it is impossible to please God" must be the perfectly free "homage of intellect and will".

By faith man is able to participate in the redemption, and redemption itself is both given and received by love. Love like faith is a free act. "When one has known the love of free man", says Péguy, "the prostrations of slaves are worthless." Through grace man is liberated from the servitude of sin and becomes a free man. He enters, says Daniélou, freedom in a new sense. "It means that man's relation to God is no longer merely that of a servant to his Lord, but also that of a son to his Father." Such a relationship is inconceivable unless it is free.

Instead, then, of basing religious liberty on social or political expediency, it can be made to depend on the nature of faith itself and to spring from it. Religious liberty is seen as the condition in which faith can achieve its purest and

fullest form. The act of faith is an interior act, but man cannot
be content with interior freedom, since he is not an anchorite
but a social being. As a human person he has to live in society
and give outward expression to his inner faith. A freedom
which cannot express itself is, in man's case, illusory. Toleration and liberty thus extend from the inner formation of faith
to its manifestations. Toleration accordingly becomes a social
policy based on the very nature of man. In a society based on
such principles religious pluralism will become the norm.
Such pluralism is not in itself desirable, but given the fallen
nature of man appears inevitable.

Religious liberty may then be considered as required by
the human person for his full development. The State, which
is little more than a mechanism to ensure the safeguarding of
the liberties of human persons and their welfare, has no right
of coercion in religious matters. The State as such has no
direct knowledge of the Church or her mission and therefore
places all religions on an equal basis, not because it considers
one to be as good as another, but because it has no means of
distinguishing between them. The State comes first in time:
the Church is first in dignity: but there is no primacy of
causality. The State is not the instrument of the Church but
has its own defined and limited functions. Given the need of
the human person for religious liberty, the State's function is
to safeguard it, and not to impede man as he pursues his end
of moving freely towards God.

Intolerance does have a place in religion, but it is a limited
one. Within the Church there must always be a dogmatic intolerance arising from the Church's mission as teacher of the
truth and guardian of the deposit of faith. The Church is
bound to defend the truth entrusted to her, but she carries
out her duties with prudence and charity. When she must she
resorts to her weapon of excommunication, a spiritual not a
temporal weapon. In the world, however, the Church has to
co-exist with other faiths: a necessity which will grow more
imperative as the rudiments of a world order are formed and

a genuine international society created. She has to lead men to truth not by the exercise of a coercive will but by persuasion. To fulfil this mission she needs freedom but nothing more. "It is not the office of the Church", declared Pius XII in his address to the new cardinals on February 20th, 1946, "to include and in a manner embrace, like a gigantic world empire, all human society. This concept of the Church as earthly empire and worldly domination is fundamentally false. She follows in her progress and her expansion an opposite path to that of modern imperialism. She progresses before all else in depth, then in extension. She seeks primarily man himself.... Her work is completed in the depths of each man's heart, but it has its own repercussions on all the duration of life, on all the fields of activity of each one. With men so formed the Church prepares for human society a base on which it can rest with security."

CHAPTER II

LAW AND MORALS

Modern society is essentially pluralist in its religious construction with men of different religious faiths owing a common allegiance to the State. In such a situation law cannot be co-extensive with morals since from different religious premises different moral judgements will flow, and it is obvious they cannot all be enforced by law. In any case, it would be widely agreed within the Western tradition that there are intrinsic differences between law and morality although their spheres overlap. The connection between morality and the criminal law has been particularly close. All serious crimes are also moral offences, and the notion of personal responsibility which informs the criminal law was a principle of moral theology before it was accepted into the law. *Actus non facit reum nisi mens sit rea*: the act and the intention must concur to constitute the crime.

The most important and obvious difference between law and morality lies in the sanctions imposed. In law the sanction is essentially physical and external, consisting in a fine or the deprivation of liberty or even, in certain cases, of life itself. The sanction is imposed collectively in the name of society after a formal judicial process. The moral sanction is primarily interior and imposed not by the courts but by conscience. In morality much stress is laid on motives, but these are secondary where the law is concerned. The law requires the establishment of a criminal intention, but this is ascertained not by interior inquisition but by external evidence.

A further point of differentiation is one of scope. Law is concerned primarily with the general good of the community while morality goes beyond this to consider the individual good. Law enforces only those standards of moral behaviour indispensable for community existence whereas morality calls for conformity with the ideal. The man who limited himself to the minimum moral requirements laid down by the law would not be the good man of the Western and Christian tradition. Morality, especially Catholic moral theology, is an exact science whereas law, and in particular the criminal law, lacks the comprehensiveness of a moral code. Offences have been created in a haphazard fashion to meet particular social needs and not to accord with preconceived doctrine.

These distinctions are not absolute, but one would hardly expect them to be since the connection between law and morals is in fact close. This factual connection makes the rigid distinction between law and morals elaborated by positivist jurists such as Austin and Bentham unreal. Austin defined law purely by reference to its form with no reference to morality whatsoever. Law, he maintained, was the command of a sovereign superior laid down to an inferior and backed by a sanction for disobedience. An important objection to this approach, which is said to have the merit of clarity, is that it leaves the individual helpless before the law. If law is constituted purely by form, on what basis can the citizen resist an unjust law? The point is far from academic. Hitler came to power by legal means and used the machinery of the law and the courts to destroy the liberal basis of German society, a task in which he was greatly aided by the dominance of Positivist thought in pre-war German legal thinking.

In any case Positivism must be rejected since it does not accord with the social facts. In Western society the connection between law and the moral sense of the community is as real as its connection with a sanction. Law is obeyed by the majority as much because it is felt to be morally binding as because of the knowledge that a breach of it will lead to punishment. Exceptions exist to this statement such as customs laws, but they are minor. Law does not exist in isolation but is an institution reflecting the life and views of society. When it ceases to correspond with the underlying beliefs and habits of a people it ceases to be enforceable. The law relating to obscene books provides a good example of the influence of moral ideas upon the law. What was considered obscene in the nineteenth century is freely publishable today because the moral ideas of the English-speaking peoples have changed in the meantime. The same is true of the law governing contraceptive information. In the seventies of the last century books imparting such information were considered obscene but they are no longer subject to legal action now that contraception is generally accepted in the community. Yet there has been no formal change in the law.

Catholic thought on the relation between law and morals, and the character and function of the State, has been built up on Aristotelian foundations, regarding the State as a natural and good institution, essential for the full development of man, who is by nature a social animal, and is therefore charged with a duty to promote virtue. On the other hand Protestant thinking about the State and its functions is essentially Augustinian, looking upon the State as an institution permeated by evil, essential to check vice but competent to do little else.

St Thomas Aquinas developed a comprehensive philosophy of the State and of law whose influence on Catholic thinking has been profound. For St Thomas as for Aristotle the State was a good and natural institution designed to lead the citizen to virtue. The State was a perfect society in its own right, deriving authority from God through the structure of human nature itself. All law came from God and was known in two ways, through direct revelation, the divine law, or through human reason, the natural law. "Now among all others, the rational creature is subject to Divine Providence in the most excellent way, in so far as it partakes of a share of providence, by being provident for itself and others. Wherefore it has a share of the Eternal Reason, whereby it has a natural inclination to its proper act and end: and this participation of the eternal law in the rational creature is called the natural law."[1] The two could not conflict since they were alternative modes of apprehending the law of God. Positive law derived from natural law and if in conflict with it possessed no validity. An unjust law was "no law at all".

An objection to the Thomist system is that it may by putting forward a purposive interpretation of law threaten human freedom and human dignity. This objection can hardly be sustained when the limited character of the Thomist view of law is considered. He defines law as "an ordinance of reason for the common good, made by him who has care of the community and has promulgated (it)". The common good was not an abstract concept such as the greatest good of the greatest number but a common good of persons, and the nature of the human person limited the function of law. Furthermore, the law was not to promote every virtue nor to suppress every vice. It was to forbid only those vices from which it was possible for the majority of imperfect human beings to abstain "and chiefly those that are to the hurt of others, without the prohibition of which society could not be maintained: thus human law prohibits murder, theft and suchlike". Human law "does not prescribe concerning all the acts of every virtue: but only in regard to those that are ordainable to the common good—either immediately, as when certain things are done directly for the common good—or mediately as when a lawgiver prescribes certain things pertaining to good order, whereby the citizens are directed in the upholding of the common good of justice and peace".[2]

Protestant theologians are for the most part profoundly unsympathetic to the natural law approach. For the Catholic the

[1] *Summa Theologica*, Ia–IIae, qu. 91, art. 2.
[2] *Summa Theologica*, Ia–IIae, qu. 16, art. 3.

State would have been necessary for man had he remained a perfect being; for the Protestant it is the direct result of original sin. Karl Barth goes so far as to maintain that without revelation man would be without any form of moral guidance. Reinhold Niebhur, while avoiding the extreme position of Barth, maintains that all man's rational or natural standards are involved in sin. "Undue confidence in human reason," he writes, "as the seat and source of natural law, makes this very concept of law into a vehicle of human sin. It gives to the peculiar conditions and unique circumstances in which reason operates in a particular historical moment the sanction of universality."[3] In place of the natural law with its detailed deductions he substitutes the Lutheran idea of the order of creation. This "limits the law to a natural fact, such as natural bisexuality for instance, and does not introduce some specious universality of reason. It is not possible to escape the natural fact that the primary purpose of bisexuality in nature is that of procreation. But it is not easy to establish a universally valid 'law of reason' which will eternally set the bounds for the function of sex in the historic development of human personality."

The Protestant approach to morality is characterized not only by a rejection of natural law but by an emphasis on the rôle of ethics as a critical inquiry into concrete problems of the moral life rather than the formulation of abstract rules of conduct. Thus in his book *Morals and Medicine*, Joseph Fletcher, a Protestant clergyman, writes: "Deliberately we have relied upon a cumulative support for our central thesis, choosing to bring out what it means in a clinical style by examining concrete problems rather than by presenting a contrived and systematic construction of ethical doctrine." Protestant morality is thus an "ethic of inspiration" rather than an "ethic of ends". Unlike the morality based on natural law, which is a fully developed system resulting from rational reflection on man's nature, his relationship to society, and the

[3] *The Nature and Destiny of Man*, I, 298.

rôle of the State, Protestant morality is an attitude towards life. It is based on a confrontation of persons, the meeting of the individual and his Lord, an experience rather than a rational working out of abstractions of justice.

It is clear that the Protestant approach to morality will give much less guidance in shaping the law in relation to morals than that of the Catholic. Yet both Protestant and Catholic have a common interest in the regulation of power by morality. Can some principle be found acceptable to both which will mark out the frontiers between law and morality and in particular draw a line between morality and the criminal law? In the United States the formulation of such a principle is complicated by the tendency of modern American jurisprudence to regard the State as a natural agency separate from the Church in both its secular function and its lack of subordination to the divine positive law. The accompanying disposition to regard the enforcement of merely moral precepts, the infraction of which is not harmful to the peace of the community, as beyond the power of the State, is shown in the American treatment of sumptuary laws. The laws restricting the sale or use of contraceptives have all but disappeared. Moreover, even the United States Government is now disseminating birth control information through its agencies of foreign aid. On the other hand, there are areas of American life where, partly due to the influence of the puritan strain in American law and partly due to the imperatives of preserving order, the law does undertake to enforce precepts of morality. Examples are found in the generally negative attitude of the law towards artificial human insemination, human sterilization, homosexuality, suicide and euthanasia. But even where the positive law coincides in its commands with the prevalent precepts of morality, it is characteristic of American legal thought to search for a neutral, secular justification for the law. So, with the Sunday-closing laws, the Supreme Court sustained them, against constitutional attack as laws respecting an establishment of religion, only because, whatever may have been the religious character of their inception, they had long since ceased to have a religious purpose. Now, felt the Court, they were merely secular laws mandating, for secular reasons, one day of rest in seven. A similar analysis undoubtedly would be applied to any other sumptuary laws which should happen to come before it. It is significant, though, that no principled rationale of the relation between law and morality in these areas has yet been authoritatively formulated.

In Great Britain the attempt to establish such a general principle was made by the Wolfenden Committee in its report on Homosexual Offences and Prostitution published in 1957. The committee concluded that the function of the criminal law in those fields "is to preserve order and decency, to protect the citizen from what is offensive or injurious, and to provide sufficient safeguards against the exploitation and corruption of others, particularly those who are specially vulnerable because they are young, weak in body or mind, inexperienced, or in a state of special physical, official or economic dependence". It went on to draw a sharp distinction between crime which comes within the sphere of the law and sin, which is confined to the realm of private morality. "There must", said the report, "remain a realm of private morality and immorality which is, in brief and crude terms, not the law's business." The committee's statement of principle was made in relation to a limited subject matter, but it is clearly applicable to the whole field of criminal law. The opinion of the committee had been anticipated by John Stuart Mill in his book *On Liberty*, where he writes: "The only purpose for which power can rightfully be exercised over any member of a civilized community against his will is to prevent harm to others.... His own good either physical or moral is not a sufficient warrant. He cannot rightfully be compelled to do or forbear because it will be better for him to do so, because it will make him happier, because in the opinions of others, to do so would be wise or even right." He exempted from this doctrine children and backward societies and it was to apply only to men "in the maturity of their faculties".

The Mill–Wolfenden view on the legal enforcement of morality has received support from Professor H. L. A. Hart in his recent book *Law, Liberty and Morality*.[4] In it he argued that punishment of an offender always involves deprivation of liberty or property, the infliction of pain on the individual, and therefore requires some special justification. The second effect of legal enforcement is to deter others from offending against the law, who are coerced into obedience by the threat of legal punishment. Professor Hart condemns such coercion, especially in the sexual sphere, since sexual impulses are a normal part of daily life and repression may result in the distortion of the individual's emotional life, happiness and personality. Finally he denies that any significance can be attached to the fact that certain conduct is prohibited by positive morality. "The utilitarian denies that this has any significance sufficient to justify its enforcement; his opponent asserts that it has."

Here certainly is a fundamental point of divergence. The utilitarian view is too narrow in its scope because it excludes all question of positive morality. Yet the moral laws of a community are relevant to its general welfare and should not therefore be excluded in advance from all consideration of law enforcement. In any case it is a fact that the law has developed in accordance with the community's moral ideas. As has been pointed out, most criminal offences are also moral offences and moral responsibility is an essential element of criminal law. Furthermore, the distinction between crime and sin is not the appropriate one to draw. Sin, as such, is a theological concept, jurisdiction over which is confined to the Church. The State knows nothing of sin as sin, but it may well be concerned with conduct contrary to the moral standards accepted by the community which may incidentally be sinful.

Lord Devlin in his lecture "The Enforcement of Morals",

[4] London: Oxford University Press, 1963.

given to the British Academy in 1959, rejects the Wolfenden view. There can be, he states, no theoretical limits set to the State's power to legislate against immorality. He reaches this conclusion by answering two questions. First, has society the right to pass judgement on matters of morals? Second, if society has the right to pass judgement, has it also the right to use the weapon of the law to enforce it? He answers the first question in the affirmative on the basis that a recognized morality is essential to the continued existence of society, and then maintains that the answer to the first question "may very well dictate" an answer to the second. It is not clear whether Lord Devlin is saying that morality should be enforced to preserve society or whether he is saying that the enforcement of morality by law is a justifiable end in itself, but on either basis there is a gap in the argument. The conclusion that society has the right to enforce moral judgements by law does not flow from the premise that it has the right to pass them. To maintain this is both to ignore the limited character of law and to leave no basis of right for Church, conscience or individual liberty.

Lord Devlin's views have received some support from the case of *Shaw* v. *Director of Public Prosecutions* of 1961 where Lord Mansfield's dictum of 1774 was quoted with approval by some of the judges: "Whatever is *contra bonos mores et decorum*, the principles of our laws prohibit and the King's Court as the general censor and guardian of the public morals is bound to restrain and punish." Shaw had published a magazine called the *Ladies Directory*, a directory of the names and addresses of various prostitutes, and was charged among other things with a conspiracy to corrupt public morals. This offence which was thought by many to have fallen into desuetude was revived by the House of Lords in order to constitute itself the overseer of the morals of the nation. The Lord Chancellor put forward a sweeping claim:

When Lord Mansfield, speaking long after the Star Chamber had been abolished, said that the Court of King's Bench was the *custos morum* of the people and had the superintendency of offences *contra bonos mores*, he was asserting, as I now assert, that there is in that Court a residual power, where no statute has yet intervened to supersede the common law, to superintend those offences which are prejudicial to the public welfare. Such occasions will be rare, for Parliament has not been slow to legislate when attention has been sufficiently aroused. But gaps remain and will always remain, since no one can foresee every way in which the wickedness of man may disrupt the order of society.... Let it be supposed that at some future, perhaps early, date, homosexual practices between adult consenting males are no longer a crime. Would it not be an offence if even without obscenity such practices were publicly advocated and encouraged by pamphlet and advertisement? Or must we wait till Parliament finds time to deal with such conduct? I say, my Lords, that if the common law is powerless in such an event then we should no longer do her reverence. But I say that her hand is still powerful and that it is for her Majesty's Judges to play the part which Lord Mansfield pointed out to them.

This sort of claim is foreign to the common law tradition which places a high value on the close definition of offences. Nor has the common law seen much virtue in the enforcement of morality as such but has always sought for some particular harm to the community before it has created a new offence. Thus in Curl's case in 1727, when the common law courts were assuming jurisdiction over obscene literature, the Attorney-General when urging the point was careful to limit his argument: "I do not insist that every immoral act is indictable such as telling a lie or the like; but if it is destructive of morality in general, if it does, or may, affect all the King's subjects, it is then an offence of a publick nature. And upon this distinction it is, that particular acts of fornication are not punishable in the Temporal Courts and bawdy-houses are."

One may say, then, disagreeing with both Lord Devlin and Sir John Wolfenden, that a theoretical principle limiting enforcement of morals by law can be erected, a principle derived in part from Thomist teaching and in part from the experience of the common law, namely, that those moral offences which affect the common good are fit subjects for legislation. This is not to say that every moral offence affecting the common good will be made a crime but only that it may be so treated. Moral offences not affecting the common welfare should be excluded from the scope of the law.

It is clearly necessary to define what is meant by the common good. Public order and civil peace: the security of the young, the weak and the inexperienced, the maintenance of the decencies of public behaviour, all are included within the concept of the common good. These ideas do not exhaust it. Every community holds certain moral ideas and ideals of behaviour in common, and this moral consensus also forms part of the common good. In preserving this consensus the law probably has a minor rôle to play: of much greater importance are the forces of education and persuasion and of actual behaviour in society, but one cannot exclude the law altogether. The consensus is more likely to be affected by public than by private acts, but one cannot say arbitrarily that no private act can ever affect the common good. Artificial insemination by a donor is a private act but it may have profound effects on the status of the family in society. Equally, euthanasia takes place in private but the acceptance of euthanasia as legitimate might well modify the principle of the sanctity of life held in common by society.

Whether behaviour, public or private, strikes at the common good in such a manner that it endangers the fabric of society, and so should be suppressed by law, is a question of fact, which can only be answered after a full consideration of the conditions prevailing in a given society and the relevant jurisprudential, sociological and psychological data involved. Even then it does not follow that the law should necessarily be invoked. It may not be enforceable, or not enforceable equitably, or may give rise to greater evils than those it is intended to eradicate.

One can learn nothing of its ultimate validity from this

conception of the common good. It has been used not in the ideal sense of what is in accordance with right reason, but rather in Newman's sense of what is the "common possession" of society. In his *Historical Sketches* he writes: "Next I lay down, that, whereas a State is in its very idea a society, and a society is a collection of many individuals made one by their participation in some common possession, and to the extent of that common possession, the presence of that possession held in common constitutes the life, and the loss of it constitutes the dissolution of a State." It is through this medium of the "common possession" that natural law concepts operate, not through the imposition from above of a body of abstract rules. Much of the current writing on natural law from Catholic sources appears to be nothing more than rhetoric with neither social nor legal effect. The law is nothing else than the collective conscience of the community on those issues which cannot be left to individual choice. In so far as the community is faithful to the Western and Christian tradition it may reflect higher norms, but there can be no certainty that it will do so. The law systematizes consciences and to that extent has moral authority, but consciences can err and the law cannot guarantee rightness.

How does one assess what in fact are the prevailing moral views in the community? One can, of course, look to the law itself, and Mr Richard O'Sullivan[5] has devoted considerable scholarship to showing how far common law notions have a Christian foundation. But this approach is helpful only up to a point. The preservation of a moral judgement in the law is no indication that the view is still generally held in society. A better guide than the letter of the law is the manner and spirit of its enforcement, and time and again a law out of accord with current moral sentiment has been rendered nugatory, not by repeal but by non-enforcement. The law recognizes moral values not only in what it commands and punishes but in what it refuses to countenance. Contracts

[5] *Inheritance of Common Law*; see Select Bibliography.

made for an immoral purpose are not enforceable at law. Agreements which prejudice public safety, the administration of justice, or the status of marriage, are treated as being contrary to public policy and held void. Adultery, prostitution, homosexual relationships are not recognized as sources of rights by the law.

Lord Devlin instructs us to take as our criterion for the moral judgement of society "something about which any twelve men or women drawn at random might after discussion be expected to be unanimous". This is not especially helpful where controversial moral questions are concerned, for these are precisely the issues on which society has ceased to have a unanimous opinion. He also warns against dismissing expressions of disgust as tests of moral sentiment, on the grounds that they are indications that the limits of toleration have been reached. These expressions may be of some utility in assessing the emotional content of moral opinion, but they cannot, as he seems to suggest, be a basis for penal policy in a society which maintains any claim to rationality. There are also the dubious aids of the sociologists and the pollsters. At some time in the future the techniques of social research may have been so developed that they will prove reliable guides, but at the present time they are the subject of acrimonious professional dispute.

The conclusions offered by Dr Kinsey and others are not especially enlightening. Dr Kinsey certainly established that the variations from the norm of sexual behaviour in American society were very much more widespread than had previously been supposed, but one can no more conclude from his findings that people believed such aberrations to be right, even if they practised them, than one can conclude that because aberrations exist they are therefore right in themselves. On this last point, the Catholic will find the Kinsey reports no more than somewhat distressing glosses on the Church's doctrine of original sin. Polls of public opinion with their loaded questions, limited scope and snap responses are even less reliable as guides to ethical views. Perhaps the best guide to moral opinion is found in those agencies which are influential in forming society's views such as the Churches, Parliament, professional bodies and the press. This is a rough and ready guide, but there appears to be no better.

A pluralist society in which divergent views are held on religion and morality may or may not be a higher achievement than a unitary society where only one faith prevails, but it is the type of modern society and likely to be that of the future. In such societies moral conclusions and policies with moral implications are not laid down from above but are gradually evolved through the discussions of free men. Law is not simply equated with force or with the majority will but is limited by the rights of the human person, the status of non-governmental institutions and the consensus of moral ideas. Faced with the threat of a corrosive agnosticism, the Christian, aware of his minority position, seeks an ally in the law, since the law may well preserve moral ideas long after the theology or moral views which gave rise to it have passed away. The law's view, for example, that the contract of marriage creates a permanent status and is not dissoluble by mutual consent is founded on Christian principles. "It has got there", as Lord Devlin stresses, "because it is Christian, but it remains there because it is built into the house in which we live and could not be removed without bringing it down." In 1963 Mr Leo Abse sought to alter the law fundamentally by introducing a private member's Bill into the House of Commons, which would have allowed the dissolution of a marriage after seven years, if it could be established that the marriage had irretrievably broken down. This would have introduced an entirely new principle into the marriage law, and with Christian opposition the proposal was defeated. The Christian attempt to preserve moral values by supporting existing institutions is understandable and in many cases reasonable. It ceases to be so when the moral judgement expressed by the law no longer has any correspondence with the prevailing view of society. In pluralist societies where there is only a limited agreed morality, only what is generally agreed can be part of the public moral order. Where there is no consensus the question must be left to be determined in the private sphere. As Newman has written, it is imperative that "public opinion should give the law to law". The Church may be assured of her own rightness and claims but cannot act as though these were recognized in full by civil society. Her minimum requirement, which may possibly be enough, is that on issues where agreement is impossible her members should not be bound by the State to act in violation of their consciences.

The Church has the right to make use of all the democratic processes to let her views be known, but it is wisdom to recognize that in the sphere of morals the law can only have a minor rôle to play. Of much greater importance are the forces of persuasion and education and the preservation of morality in the social fabric, and it is in this sphere that the principal contribution of the Church can be made.

CHAPTER III

CAPITAL PUNISHMENT, SUICIDE AND EUTHANASIA

CAPITAL PUNISHMENT

The traditional Christian view on capital punishment is that the State has the right to take life but that it should be invoked only in the case of grave crimes. In the American States, the major capital crimes, in terms of the number of States involved, are, in addition to murder: kidnapping, rape, treason, robbery, lynching, crimes of extreme danger to life, train-wrecking, arson, perjury resulting in the execution of an innocent party and certain types of aggravated assaults. There are also specialized capital offences in the military services. Under English law capital punishment applies to only four offences, murder, treason, piracy and arson of a royal ship or dockyard. Treason in peacetime is a very rare offence: and in the case of piracy and arson of a royal ship, the offender is automatically reprieved. In practice, then, murder is the only offence to attract the death penalty under English law. The justification of the traditional Christian position is the idea of retribution. Murder is considered one of the gravest of crimes, a violation of the commandment "Thou shalt not kill". Retribution is used here not in the sense of satisfying personal feelings of vindictiveness but in the sense of there being a personal responsibility in the case of a man who commits a grave crime who can only expiate his guilt by undergoing punishment. This theory of retribution does not of necessity require that the death penalty be imposed for murder, but only that there be some proportion between the crime committed and the punishment imposed. A serious crime should not be visited with a trivial penalty and correspondingly a minor crime should not be the subject of draconian punishment.

Retribution is, however, used in a second sense of satisfying outraged moral feelings, and in this form has been put forward as a justification for capital punishment for the crime of murder. So, Lord Denning, in his evidence to the Royal Commission on Capital Punishment, said: "The punishment for grave crimes should adequately reflect the revulsion felt by the majority of citizens for them. It is a mistake to consider the object of punishment as being deterrent or reformative or preventive and nothing else. The ultimate justification of any punishment is not that it is a deterrent but that it is the emphatic denunciation by the community of a crime and from this point of view there are some murders which in the present state of opinion demand the death penalty." The Lord Chancellor in the House of Lords debate of July 1956 agreed with this view, and it was also supported by Archbishop Fisher in the evidence he gave to the Royal Commission. It is, however, open to serious objection on two grounds. In the first place it is an emotional rather than a rational argument. Secondly it does not in fact justify the death penalty since "emphatic denunciation" does not require the imposition of this particular form of suffering. As Professor Hart has stated: "The normal way in which moral condemnation is expressed is by *words*, and it is not clear, if denunciation is really what is required, why a solemn public statement of disapproval would not be the most 'appropriate' or 'emphatic' means of expressing this. Why should a denunciation take the form of punishment?"[1]

[1] *Law, Liberty and Morality*, p. 66.

Retribution apart, capital punishment is justified by Christians and others on the ground that it is necessary for the defence of society. An individual has the right to defend his life against an unjust aggressor and also those lives committed to his care. He may under English law even take the life of the aggressor but only if it is the one means by which his life may be defended. The same argument applies to the State, which is under a duty to protect the lives of its citizens. One must therefore ask the question whether the death penalty is necessary for the defence of society? It might be thought a simple matter to look at those countries which have abolished the death penalty—which include the majority of those in Europe and about nine American States—and see whether the murder rate has risen or not after abolition. Unfortunately social and other conditions vary so much from one country to another, and abolition has usually been preceded by a long period of disuse of the death penalty so that it is impossible to draw any firm conclusions. Contiguous States in the United States and New Zealand in some of which the death penalty has been abolished and in others in which it has not provide a better basis for assessment, and the Royal Commission on Capital Punishment was able to conclude that the murder rate in death penalty and abolitionist States was conditioned by factors other than the death penalty.

If the death penalty is considered by itself, the fact that it is more savage than other penalties would seem to indicate that it is in fact a unique deterrent. Yet such an isolated approach is not justifiable. The effectiveness of a deterrent depends as much on the certainty of its imposition as on the nature of the penalty itself, and it is this uncertainty, the chance of getting away with it, which makes it less of a deterrent to a potential murderer. One must also consider who the people are who are being deterred. Murder is largely the crime of insane or unbalanced people.

Between 1900 and 1949, 4,842 murderers were known to the police and, of these, 1,712 committed suicide before arrest, a fact which in itself suggests an unbalanced mind. Of the remainder committed for trial, 1,400 were found insane. Thus, over half a century, the majority of murderers appear to some degree to have been of unsound mind. The same story is told by the Home Office report on murder of 1961, showing that a third of murderers committed suicide after the crime. In the three years 1958, 1959 and 1960 nearly a third of those prosecuted for murder were found insane. Sex-murderers are unlikely to be guided by rational considerations and the same is true of any murder where passion plays a part. The Home Office report of 1961 indicated that many murders are committed within the family, and here again emotional factors would be dominant.

Far from deterring murder, in some cases the death penalty acts as an incitement. The trial for life with its accompanying drama attracts a certain type of psychopathic personality. It may also be stated more generally that the death penalty reduces the reverence for life in the community and therefore prepares the ground for murder.[2]

That the death penalty is a deterrent is obvious: that it is a unique and necessary deterrent is open to grave question. In any case the deterrent argument for the Christian must always be a limited one, since it is one that treats the human being as a means rather than an end. As Sir Walter Moberly has written: "the characteristic Christian attitude to all men, however ill they have behaved, is redemptive. For Christians legitimate punishment will normally be a family affair. Its aim will include the correction of the wrongdoer who is seen as an erring son rather than a 'public enemy'. *Prima facie* capital punishment is un-Christian, since its object is to end the criminal and not mend him."

[2] "I believe", said Archbishop Temple, "that the example of the State taking life, even when it only does so in return for a life already taken, does more to lower the value of human life in the minds of its citizens than the deterrent influence of this penalty can do to protect the lives of the citizens."

A further objection to the death penalty is its finality. If by some chance a mistake is made, it cannot be rectified. Mistakes have been made in other branches of the criminal law where men have been convicted for crimes they were afterwards found not to have committed, and there seems no reason why this should not occur in the case of murder.

In England in the case of Timothy Evans, who was hanged in 1950, it may well have happened. Chief witness for the prosecution was a man John Christie, who later turned out to be a mass murderer. He lived in the same house as Evans, and at his trial Evans had accused him of murdering his wife. The bodies of six women were found in Christie's flat and backyard strangled in the same way as Mrs Evans. In 1955 Mr Chuter Ede, Home Secretary at the time that Evans was tried, admitted that he had made a mistake in signing the execution papers for Evans.

The moral effect of an execution upon those who have to witness it is another reason for rejecting the death penalty. The brutalizing effect on the executioner is obvious, and according to one Prison Commissioner five applications a week are received for the post. The Reverend S. R. Glanville Murray, a prison chaplain, speaks of the harm to the physical and mental health of those who witness executions: "An execution is a moral shock of such a nature that it is impossible to say what may be its ultimate effects on mind and body." The interest shown by the public who flock either to the trial or to the prison where the murderer is due to be executed is also morbid and undesirable.

A final argument against the death penalty is that it is out of accord with the whole modern development of the penal system with its emphasis on the reform and rehabilitation of the criminal. Probation has increased steadily in importance as a means of dealing with criminals: after-care has been developed. In the United States, increased consideration is being given, in legal and penological circles, to the employment of life sentences and corrective treatment of mental disturbances, coupled with improved parole techniques, as an alternative to capital punishment. Parole is a necessary corollary to the life sentence approach, and it is rare that a criminal sentenced to life imprisonment will actually serve the remainder of his days in prison. Significantly, several studies in American jurisdictions indicate that the release on parole of life sentence prisoners can be accomplished, given appropriate procedural and supervisory safeguards, without an undue risk to the public. Under the British 1948 Act a special institution has been established for the detention of offenders needing psychological treatment. Open prisons are another contemporary development of great significance. Penal policy is increasingly being directed towards the end of enabling the criminal to take his place in society once again. The death penalty is in flat contradiction to this whole movement. Yet there is no reason why the murderer should not be reformed and turned into a law-abiding citizen. In only one case, that of Walter Rowland in 1947, has a reprieved and released murderer been convicted of a second similar crime.

In the early days of the American colonies, capital punishment was not as widely or as vigorously applied as it was then in England. Moreover, after the independence of the new nation was secured, some of the States enacted laws which sharply curtailed the employment of capital punishment. Later, some States began to abolish it altogether. Michigan abolished the death penalty in 1847 for all crimes except treason; and no one has since been executed in Michigan for treason. In eight other States the death penalty has been fully or virtually abolished. They, and the dates of the abolition, are: Rhode Island (1852), Wisconsin (1853), Maine (1876), Minnesota (1911), North Dakota (1915), Alaska (1957), Hawaii (1957) and Delaware (1958). Several other States have abolished capital punishment for short periods of time. (See *Comment*, "Capital Punishment", 29 Tenn. L. Rev. 534 (1962); Savitz, *Capital Crimes as Defined in American Law*, 46 J. Crim. L. 355 (1955).) In some other American jurisdictions, the death penalty, while still on the statute books, has fallen into disuse. One factor which has spurred the abolition drive has been the widespread opposition to capital punishment on the part of church leaders, including some individual Catholic clergy. It is not to be expected, however, that the campaign for the abolition of capital punishment is assured of an early, or even eventual, success. For there are indications that the arguments in favour of retention of the death penalty have considerable support, not only among the general public, but also in circles professionally concerned with the problem.

The dominant movement of the English legal system over the past century has been away from capital punishment. By the accession of Queen Victoria in 1837 the number of offences attracting the death penalty which in 1800 had been over two hundred had been reduced to fifteen. In the next twenty years or so they were reduced to the four mentioned at the opening of this chapter. In 1868 public executions were abolished after recommendations to that effect by the House of Lords and a royal commission. For the rest of the century the abolitionist movement failed to register any great success, but in 1908 the Children's Act abolished the death penalty for those under sixteen. Interest in abolition of the death penalty revived during the 1920's. The Howard League for Penal Reform, founded in 1921, had as one of its objects the abolition of the death penalty for murder, and in 1925 the National Council for the Abolition of the Death Penalty was founded. The Labour government of 1929 appointed a select committee to consider the problem which reported in favour of the suspension of the death penalty for five years. The recommendation was never put into operation.

After the war the abolitionists again became active and their hopes were raised by the return of a Labour government in 1945. When the government produced their Criminal Justice Bill in 1948 it made no mention of abolition, but an abolitionist amendment was moved by a private member and added to the Bill, only to be rejected by the House of Lords. In 1949 a royal commission was appointed to examine all questions relating to capital punishment, save the question of abolition, which was excluded from its terms of reference. Nevertheless it was evident on publication in 1953 that the report favoured abolition, and it encouraged abolitionists to resume their activities. In 1956 a private member's Bill to abolish the death penalty was passed by the Commons but was rejected by the Upper House. The government then announced that it would introduce a compromise Bill of its own which became law as the Homicide Act of 1957.

The Homicide Act abolished the death penalty for murder except for six classes of capital murder for which it was retained. The basis of the distinction was not a moral but a social one, capital punishment being retained for those classes of murder for which it was thought to be necessary and believed to be a particularly effective deterrent. Any murder done in course or furtherance of a theft attracts the death penalty, as does a murder by shooting or causing an explosion. A murder done in the course of resisting arrest or escaping from legal custody is capital, as is the murder of a police officer acting in the execution of his duty. Prisoners who murder prison officers are also subject to the death penalty. Finally, anyone who commits a second or subsequent murder on an occasion different from the first is capitally punished.

The Homicide Act has created an anomalous situation by its ignoring of the variation in moral heinousness of different types of murder. A murder during a petty theft carries the death penalty while one committed in the course of a rape does not. Its basic principle of deterrence has been undermined by evidence which shows that murder in course of theft has gone up by considerably more than any non-capital murder. Since it can hardly be seriously argued that a return should be made to the *status quo* before the Act, the logical course would be to abolish the death penalty altogether. This should be welcomed by Christians, who should be predisposed by their religion to a reformative view of punishment.

Capital punishment has been the source of lively controversy among Christians but they have been unanimous in condemning suicide as a grave offence against God. In this Christianity confirms a basic human impulse of self-preservation. Even in the ancient world suicide was condemned by the majority. Both Thebes and Athens denied funeral rites to suicides, and Attic law directed that the hand of a suicide should be cut off and buried away from the rest of the body. Plato condemned suicide in general although he allowed some exceptions, and Aristotle thought it an act of cowardice and an offence against the State. Minority schools of philosophers such as the Epicureans and the Stoics approved of suicide, but this did not become the dominant view. Roman law contained no general prohibition of suicide, although it did punish it in individual instances. A soldier who committed suicide to avoid military duty was guilty of infamous conduct; and if he made an unsuccessful attempt, was punished with death. Roman writers expressed differing views. In different degrees Virgil, Apuleius, Caesar and Ovid condemned suicide. Cicero disapproved of it on religious and social grounds. By contrast the Roman Stoics thought suicide a basic human right. "Human affairs", reflected Seneca, "are in such a happy situation that no one need be wretched but by choice. Do you like to be wretched? Live. Do you like it not? It is in your power to return from whence you came."

SUICIDE

The Christian doctrine on suicide was formulated by St Augustine in *The City of God* and by other early Fathers of the Church. Augustine's first ground for condemning suicide was that it violated the commandment "Thou shalt not kill", which applied to all innocent lives, one's own as much as another's. His second ground for condemnation was that by its very nature it excluded any opportunity for repentance. Finally, he stigmatized it as a cowardly act. Affliction should be borne in the manner of Job. Those virgins who took their own lives to save their virtue were in error, since chastity was a virtue of the mind and could not be lost by assault. Augustine also condemned the practice of the Circumcellions, a sect whose members took their own lives in order to avoid the defilement of sin.

Church law came to reflect Augustine's views. In the fifth century the Council of Arles (452) condemned suicide. The Auxerre Synod of 578 laid down that no offering should be accepted from a suicide. In 563 the Council of Braga restricted the funeral rites that were allowed to suicides and the *Capitula* of Theodore, Archbishop of Canterbury, laid down that Mass was not to be said for suicides. The Council of Toledo (693) punished attempted suicide by exclusion from the fellowship of the Church for two months. The Synod of Nîmes in 1284 refused to allow suicides to be buried in consecrated ground. The Church thus left her severe condemnation of suicide in no doubt.

St Thomas Aquinas and other scholastics elaborated Church doctrine on suicide during the Middle Ages. St Thomas condemned suicide because it was opposed to nature and to proper self-love. He added that God alone had control over life and death, and in deciding the moment of his own death the suicide was taking over the power of God. He also condemned suicide as an offence against the community, by depriving it of one of its members. On suicide to preserve chastity, he follows the opinion of Augustine and like him allows one exception to his condemnation, those who, like Samson, took their lives under divine inspiration.

The teaching of St Augustine and St Thomas is the foundation of contemporary Catholic moral attitudes to suicide. It is condemned as a violation of the commandment "Thou shalt not kill", as contrary to nature, a usurpation of God's prerogative and a social wrong. Catholic canon law penalizes both suicide and its attempt. Canon 985 imposes "irregularity" for attempted suicide: canon 1240 denies ecclesiastical burial to those who commit suicide *deliberato consilio* and canon 1241 forbids the offering of Mass for them. Anglican canon law does not explicitly penalize suicide but excludes from Christian burial those guilty of "crime without repentance". Christian thought allows certain exceptions to its general condemnation of suicide. That covered by divine inspiration has been noted. Another exception arises where suicide is the method imposed by the State for the execution of a just death penalty. A third exception is altruistic suicide, where the intention is not to take one's own life but to save another's. The best known example is that of Captain Oates, who walked out of his camp into the Arctic wastes in order to give his companions a better chance to survive.

English law was deeply influenced by the Christian attitude to suicide. Originally jurisdiction was exercised by the ecclesiastical courts which enforced the general canon law of the Church condemning suicide, accepted into England during the seventh century. The penalty of denial of burial rites was specifically laid down in a canon of King Edgar of 967. The further punishment of dishonouring the corpse owed nothing to the Church but was based on popular custom, and this became incorporated into the common law. In his *Commentaries* Blackstone lays down that burial was to be in the highway, not in the churchyard, and that a stake was to be driven through the body. Corpses of suicides were often buried at crossroads so that the evil influence of the body could be dissipated. Burial might not take place during daylight hours but had to be carried out at night. These customs were followed throughout the eighteenth century and aroused no condemnation. In 1784 John Wesley is found writing to Pitt, urging him to discourage suicide by hanging the suicide's corpse in chains. By the first part of the nineteenth century the practice began to fall into desuetude, the last to be recorded being that of Griffiths in 1823 who was buried at a crossroads but without a stake. In 1824 a statute abolished the practice but laid down that burial was to be at night and without religious ceremony.

Suicides were also subject to forfeiture of land or goods. Edgar's canon of 967 provides that a suicide's goods shall be forfeited to his lord unless he was actuated by madness or illness. Bracton, in the mid-thirteenth century, seems to have been doubtful about the precise status of the rule, but concludes that if the suicide were committed to avoid punishment or conviction for felony then his lands escheat and his chattels are forfeited. The same results if he committed suicide without any cause. If, however, he committed suicide from "weariness of life or impatience of pain", then the lands descend to his heir and only his chattels are forfeited. If he was insane at the time, he lost neither. The practice of forfeiting chattels in all cases where a sane man committed suicide gradually established itself but lands were not lost. In the eighteenth century forfeiture of goods was limited to cases where suicide was committed to avoid conviction of felony, and in 1870 it was abolished by statute.

The forfeiture of goods and chattels played an important part in the development of the law, since it led to the view that suicide was a felony, a view supported by Coke, Hale and Blackstone. In 1563 in Hale's case the judge outlined the reasons for treating suicide as a crime, which have a particular interest, since they so clearly illustrate the influence of Christianity on the law. The thought of Thomas Aquinas can clearly be seen in the judge's first reason for condemning suicide as being against nature "because it is contrary to the rules of self-preservation, which is the principle of nature, for everything living does by instinct of nature defend itself from destruction, and then to destroy one's self is contrary to nature and a thing most horrible". The influence of St Augustine is seen in the judge's second reason that suicide is an offence against God "in that it is a breach of his commandment *Thou shalt not kill*; and to kill himself by which act he kills in presumption his own soul, is a greater offence than to kill another". The judge's third reason for condemning suicide was that the king lost a subject, "he being the head has lost one of his mystical members".

Blackstone was also influenced by religious reasons in condemning suicide. "And also the law of England wisely and religiously considers, that no man hath a power to destroy life, but by commission from God, the author of it: and, as the suicide is guilty of a double offence; one spiritual in invading the prerogative of the Almighty, and rushing into his immediate presence uncalled for; the other temporal, against the king, who hath an interest in the preservation of all his subjects; the law has therefore ranked this among the highest crimes, making it a peculiar species of felony committed on one's self." He adds that an accessory before the fact is guilty of murder.

Attempted suicide was first recognized as a crime in 1854 and the practice of punishing such attempts became established. In 1879 the Criminal Code Commissioners, in their report, suggested that aiding and abetting suicide and attempts to commit suicide should be made specific statutory offences, punishable with penal servitude for life, and two years' imprisonment with hard labour respectively. These recommendations were not acted upon. In 1916 the Metropolitan Police introduced a new policy in London for dealing with attempted suicides which subsequently spread to the rest of the country. If an attempted suicide was apprehended and had relatives or friends prepared to accept responsibility for him, he was placed in their custody and no charge was preferred, unless there were special reasons for doing so, such as the commission of another crime or a previous attempt to commit suicide. Despite this policy the criminal law statistics show that a considerable number of people were sent to prison for attempted suicide. Between 1946 and 1955, 5,794 attempted suicide cases were tried by the courts, 5,477 being found guilty, and 308 sentenced to imprisonment without the option of a fine.

Participants in suicide pacts, if they survived, were formerly treated either as murderers, principals in the second degree, or accessories according to the circumstances. The Gowers committee recommended that survivors of such pacts should not be treated as murderers but should be convicted of a separate offence. It also recommended that a specific offence should be set up of aiding, abetting or instigating the suicide of another, which should be punishable with life imprisonment. A case where one party actually killed the other party would not fall within this category, and the committee concluded that it should be dealt with by the exercise of the prerogative of mercy. By the Homicide Act of 1957 the survivor of a suicide pact whether he kills the other party or not is guilty only of manslaughter.

In the United States, in most States of the Union suicide is not a crime. "Whatever may have been the law of England", said a Texas judge in 1902 in a typical statement, "or whatever that law may now be with reference to suicides, and the punishment of persons connected with suicide ... it does not obtain in Texas. So far as the law is concerned, the suicide is innocent." Other States do not go as far as this, and, while holding it to be a crime or unlawful act, declare it to be unpunishable. New York and Oregon hold that suicide is not a crime but treat it as a grave public wrong involving moral turpitude. A few States, notably Massachusetts and South Carolina, hold that suicide is a crime. In the majority of States attempted suicide is not a crime. In those States where suicide is not a crime, it might have been made a separate statutory offence, but in fact none of these States has taken this course. In a minority of States, where suicide is criminal, but not punishable, attempted suicide is a punishable crime, a position reached by interpretation of common law or statute. In States where suicide is criminal, attempted suicide constitutes a separate statutory offence. In many jurisdictions, whatever the letter of the law provides, prosecution for attempted suicide is rare. In most States suicide is a crime, either murder or a separate offence.

Does Christian doctrine require that suicide and attempted suicide should be treated as criminal offences? Traditional Christian theology has been developed on the basis that suicide is a perverse act of the will and a conscious flouting of God's authority. Insanity has been held to excuse from guilt but apart from this exception the Church has not taken into account the causes of suicide. This is hardly surprising, since it has only been comparatively recently that general medical and sociological theories of suicide have been developed and research into the problem carried out.

Those who take their lives when insane form only a small proportion of the total number of suicides, as do those who kill themselves after a rational assessment of all the factors involved. Considerable research has been carried out to explain suicides which do not fall within these two categories, and actuarialists have attempted to relate suicide to particular factors such as climate, age, sex, religion, etc. They have put forward no general theory to explain suicide. Two general schools of thought have developed, however, the sociological, where the pioneer work was carried out by Durkheim, and the psycho-analytic, following Freud. Durkheim relates suicide to social factors, egotistic suicide resulting from the lack of integration of the individual into society, the suicide rate increasing with the degree the individual is thrown on to his own resources. Altruistic suicide, on the other hand, occurs where the individual is too closely identified with society, and is too rigorously governed by custom and habit. Anomic suicide occurs amongst those whose needs are closely regulated by society and who are unable to adapt themselves when a breakdown occurs. Durkheim's theories have been borne out by subsequent research. The suicide rate in towns is higher than that in the country, and the single, widowed and divorced are more prone to suicide than the married. Investigation into the suicide rate in certain large American cities such as Chicago has shown the rate to be highest in the central, socially fluid and disorganized sectors. Sainsbury's *Suicide in London*, a study of suicide in twenty-eight London boroughs, shows a close connection between the suicide rate and the factors of social isolation and mobility.

Freud's hypothesis of a death wish in individuals has not found widespread acceptance, but his explanation of suicide as the result of long pent-up aggressive and guilt feelings, in an emotionally immature person, commands wide support. Suicide and murder on this view spring from the same impulse, but whereas in murder the aggression is turned outwards against another person, in suicide it is turned inwards against the self. In his monograph *Man Against Himself*, Karl Menninger has explored and developed this theory of suicide. A reasonable conclusion is that while attributes of personality and experience predispose to suicide, these are developed by specific social conditions. Accordingly both psychological and social factors should be taken into consideration when framing a social policy on suicide.

Research into attempted suicide has shown that many "attempts" are not so much genuine efforts to end life as appeals for help. This view has been expounded in a number of studies by Professor Stengel, Nancy Cook, J. M. A. Weiss and Moya Woodside. Professor Stengel and Miss Cook in an investigation into suicides in North London established that of the suicides investigated only a small proportion had made previous attempts, and follow-up studies of selected groups of those who have attempted suicide indicate that very few subsequently carry it out. Accordingly it seems probable that many of the cases which have come before the courts are not legal attempts at all since there was no intention of carrying out the act.

All modern research, however different its approach, indicates that the criminal law can contribute nothing to the solution of the problem of suicide. What the potential suicide needs is not punishment but help, and this the law does nothing to supply. Of course it can be said that a change in the law would be a recognition of the individualist claim that a man has the right to dispose of his own life and a denial of the Christian position that life is a trust which man holds for higher purposes. This is not a necessary implication, and a change in the law would simply indicate that the criminal law is not the best way of dealing with the problem. Nor is it likely that the repeal of criminal sanctions would lead to an increase in the number of suicides, since the abolition of an unenforceable legal rule would hardly have an effect on the deep-rooted instinct of self-preservation.

Abolition of the criminal sanction for attempted suicide is rather more important for practical purposes. As has been noted, in the past the law in England has only been enforced in a minority of cases. Attempted suicide was classed as a misdemeanour and hence no obligation existed to report it to the police. English doctors made it a practice not to do so. Nevertheless, some people were sent to prison for attempted suicide, the cases being selected on no rational principle, but through the discretionary powers of policeman or judge. A second point is the clumsiness of the law as an instrument of social policy. Attempted suicide may be nothing more than a demonstration, may be an appeal for help, or may be a genuine effort to end life, but it is virtually impossible for the courts to distinguish between these categories. Furthermore, the knowledge that attempted suicide has been a criminal offence may well discourage an attempter from seeking help, or lead his relations and friends to conceal it.

These arguments induced a special commission appointed by the Archbishop of Canterbury to recommend in 1959 that attempted suicide should cease to be a crime and that "consideration should be given" to abolishing the felony of suicide. In 1961 the government introduced a Bill into the House of Commons to abolish the criminality of suicide and attempted suicide and the Bill secured an easy passage. Aiding, abetting, counselling or procuring the suicide of another has been made a separate offence carrying a penalty of imprisonment for not more than fourteen years. This provision is in accord with Christian teaching. Christians recognize suicide as a sinful and anti-social act, and their support for change in the law is based not on individualist theory but on practical grounds. Suicide should certainly be discouraged, and the new offence does this.

With the legal question disposed of the way is open for the adoption of additional measures to prevent suicide. Under the Mental Health Act of 1959 a doctor may order that an attempter be detained in hospital or committed there, but for the section to operate there must be evidence of mental disorder and of the attempter's being a danger to himself and to others. Those who are uncertifiable and unwilling to accept help are outside the scope of the Act. This gap could be closed by giving the courts power to make temporary custody orders so that rehabilitatory treatment could be given. Psychiatric treatment should be made more easily available through local hospitals and health services. Research into the causes of suicide should be intensified, and this might well be subsidized by insurance companies as well as the government, since they have a direct financial interest in ameliorating the problem. The public should be better educated on the subject so that suicidal symptoms would be more often recognized. In the majority of cases a warning is given by the suicide before he commits the act, and if this were taken more seriously by friends and relatives, the suicide rate would be substantially reduced by the provision of psychiatric aid. Priests and ministers should be given some elementary training so as to be able to cope better with suicidal cases which they come across in the course of their ministry. Lay associations like the English "The Samaritans", the American "Save a Life League", and the suicide bureaux of the Salvation Army should expand their work of giving immediate aid to the emotionally depressed. The Swedish experiment of an emergency clinic for depression, which has been set up in Stockholm, might be imitated in other cities. In these ways some attempt could be made to tackle a pressing social problem.

EUTHANASIA

The Catholic Church has made clear that it condemns euthanasia, whether compulsory or voluntary, as a grave sin and as a violation of the right of the individual. "It is never lawful to terminate human life," said Pius XII in an address to Italian doctors in 1948, "and only the hope of safeguarding some higher good, or of preserving or prolonging this same human life, will justify exposing it to danger." In his encyclical *Mystici Corporis*, Pius XII forthrightly condemned compulsory euthanasia:

> Conscious of the obligations of our high office we deem it necessary to reiterate this grave statement today, when to our profound grief we see the bodily-deformed, the insane and those suffering from hereditary disease, at times deprived of their lives, as though they were a useless burden to society. And this procedure is hailed by some as a new discovery of human progress, and as something that is altogether justified by the common good. Yet what sane man does not recognize that this not only violates the natural and Divine law written in the hearts of every man, but flies in the face of every sensibility of civilized humanity? The blood of these victims, all the dearer to our Redeemer because deserving of greater pity, "cries to God from the earth".

The Church of England has also condemned euthanasia. Speaking in the House of Lords debate of 1936 the Archbishop of Canterbury denied that any man was entitled to take his own life, and his rejection of euthanasia was confirmed by the Archbishop of York in 1950, also speaking in the Upper House. In the same year the Church of England's Hospital Chaplain's Fellowship condemned the practice of euthanasia. In 1952 the General Convention of the Episcopal Church in

America opposed the legalizing of euthanasia "under any circumstances whatsoever".

The basis of Christian opposition to euthanasia is not that in the Christian view life has an absolute value, but that the disposal of life is in God's hands. Man has no absolute control over his life but holds it as a trust. He has the use of it but may not destroy it at will. Furthermore, Christians recognize the principle of the sanctity of life. The only occasion when a Christian may take the life of a human being is when he is an unjust aggressor against an individual or the common good.

Suffering for the Christian is not an absolute evil but has redeeming features. It may be the occasion for advancement in the spiritual life. Lord Horder in the House of Lords debate in 1950 stressed this point. "To call the function of a doctor who helps a patient to achieve that degree of elevation of spirit an intolerable burden—as the euthanasia advocate is apt to call it—seems to me to be disparaging one of the very important duties that a doctor has to perform." At the same time the Christian recognizes suffering as an evil in the natural order and is under an obligation to relieve it by moral means. Pius XII pointed out to the Italian anaesthetists in 1957 that the sick and the dying are not under a duty to endure physical suffering:

> Now the growth in the love of God and in abandonment to his will does not come from the sufferings themselves which are accepted, but from the intention in the will, supported by grace. The intention, in many of the dying, can be strengthened and become more active if their sufferings are eased, for these sufferings increase the state of weakness and physical exhaustion, check the ardour of the soul and sap the moral powers instead of sustaining them. On the other hand, the suppression of pain removes any tension in body and mind, renders prayer easy, and makes possible a more generous gift of self. If some dying persons accept their suffering as a means of expiation and a source of merits in order to go forward in

the love of God and in abandonment to his will, do not force anaesthetics on them. They should rather be aided to follow their own way. Where the situation is entirely different, it would be inadvisable to suggest to dying persons the ascetical considerations set out above, and it is to be remembered that instead of assisting towards expiation and merit, suffering can also furnish occasion for new faults.

A third cause of Christian opposition to voluntary euthanasia is that once it were admitted pressure would build up for its extension to deformed persons and imbeciles and eventually to the old and others who could be shown to be "burdens" to society. At the first annual meeting of the American Euthanasia Society in 1939 the Society's Bill for legalizing voluntary euthanasia was discussed. Some members wished to enlarge its scope and the treasurer pointed out that it was limited to voluntary euthanasia, since that was all that public opinion was prepared for. The eventual aim of the society was, he stressed, to secure the legalizing of compulsory euthanasia as well.

There is great danger in giving powers over life and death to the average physician, who may well make a mistake in diagnosis, with irreparable consequences. As Professor Yale Kamisar in his article "Some non-religious views against proposed 'mercy-killing' legislation", has pointed out: "If the range of skill and judgement among licensed physicians approaches the wide gap between the very best and the very worst members of the bar—and I have no reason to think it does not—then the minimally competent physician is hardly the man to be given responsibility for ending another's life." Lord Horder has stressed that the incurability of disease is only an estimate based upon experience, "and how fallacious experience may be in medicine only those who have had a great deal of experience fully realize". Quite apart from the possibility of error, euthanasia would destroy the confidence which exists between doctor and patient. The patient knows that the doctor will do everything possible to save his life and this plays an important part in strengthening his will to recover. Doctors themselves recognize this, and are by no means enthusiastic to be the instruments of euthanasia practices.

Despite the existence of the duty in the doctor to preserve the life of his patient, he is not under an obligation to use every conceivable means to do so. Catholic theologians express the point in the distinction they draw between ordinary and extraordinary means. Doctors are under an obligation to use the first but not the second. Ordinary means have been described as "all medicines, treatments and operations which offer a reasonable hope of benefit, and which can be obtained and used without excessive expense, pain or other inconvenience". Extraordinary means are those which do involve these factors, or which if used would not offer a reasonable hope of benefit. Of course the doctor is free to use these means if he wishes, as is the patient. The rule is one of common sense preventing a patient from reducing himself and his family to penury in pursuit of an illusory hope of recovery. The distinction is relative not absolute, and clearly what at one time would be considered an extraordinary means may well become with the advance of medical science part of normal medical routine.

The doctor may also legitimately administer drugs to relieve pain, although they may have the effect of shortening life. The patient must consent and there must be no intention on the part of the doctor to kill the patient. Speaking of drug injection to reduce pain in 1957 Pius XII said: "If there exists no direct causal link, either through the will of the interested parties or by the nature of things, between the induced unconsciousness and the shortening of life—as would be the case if the suppression of the pain could be obtained only by the shortening of life; and if, on the other hand, the actual administration of drugs brings about two distinct effects, the one the relief of pain, the other the shortening of life, the action is lawful. It is necessary, however, to observe whether there is, between these two effects, a reasonable proportion and if the advantages of one compensate for the disadvantages of the other."

Euthanasia is a crime under both American and English law. To aid another to kill himself is, as has been noted in the discussion on suicide, a special offence under English law carrying a penalty of imprisonment for a term not exceeding fourteen years. Anyone who himself administers a fatal dose to a patient is a principal in the first degree to murder whether or not the patient has given his consent. The rule is an ancient one and is found in Hales' *Pleas of the Crown*: "If a man is sick of some disease, which, by the course of nature, might possibly end his life in half a year, and another gives him a wound or hurt which hastens his death, by irritating or provoking the disease to operate more violent and speedily, this is murder or other homicide according to the circumstances in the party by whom such wound or hurt was given. For the person wounded does not die simply *ex visitatione Dei*, but his death is hastened by the hurt which he received; and the offender is not allowed to apportion his own wrong."

In practice the law is more lenient. A doctor under such circumstances would be more likely to be held guilty of manslaughter than murder. It has long been customary to reprieve those held guilty of murder by mercy killing. *The Times* in November 1946 reported the case of a man called Long who gassed his imbecile seven-year-old daughter. He was sentenced to death but reprieved a week later, with the death sentence commuted to one of life imprisonment. Another typical case was that of Mrs Brownhill in 1934. She had undergone a serious operation and was worried as to what would happen to her thirty-one-year-old imbecile son if she should not survive. As a consequence she killed him by gassing and administering aspirin. At her trial she was sentenced to death but the jury made a strong recommendation for mercy. She was reprieved two days later and after three months received a pardon.

A further way of mitigating the harshness of the law is for

juries to bring in a verdict of acquittal or to convict of a lesser offence than that charged in the indictment. In November 1962 at Liège in Belgium Madame Suzanne van de Put, her mother, her husband, her sister and her doctor, Dr Jaques Casters, were arraigned for murdering her eight-day-old daughter. Madame van de Put had taken thalidomide pills during pregnancy and her child was born with no arms or shoulder structure and with deformed feet. The accused did not deny the charge but claimed that it had been done to save the child from a life of suffering. After a trial which commanded world-wide attention the all-male jury acquitted all the defendants, despite the fact that they were clearly guilty under Belgian law. In 1947 in the United States, Repouille, an American citizen, was indicted for manslaughter in the first degree for killing his three-month-old mongol son. The jury brought in a verdict of manslaughter in the second degree and a recommendation that he be treated with the "utmost clemency". The judge imposed a nominal sentence of 5–10 years and then placed Repouille on probation. Sometimes a jury will bring in a verdict which does not accord with the facts. In 1950, for example, in another United States case, *State* v. *Sander*, the doctor indicted had admitted causing the death of a patient suffering from cancer by injecting air into the veins. This admission was denied at the trial and the jury would not recognize it as the cause of death.

The refusal of the English and American legal systems to countenance euthanasia is in accordance with the Christian principle of the sanctity of life, and the mitigation of the penalty imposed in practice accords with Christian charity. This position has not satisfied a minority who for many years have worked for the legalizing of euthanasia. In England the contemporary euthanasia movement dates from 1936 when the Voluntary Euthanasia Legalization Society was formed under the presidency of Lord Moynihan, a former president of the Royal College of Surgeons. The Society sponsored a Bill legalizing euthanasia which was introduced into the Lords in the same year, and was rejected. The Lords returned to the subject in 1950 but only a handful of peers could be found to speak in its favour. In 1938, an American society, similar to that in England, was formed by an American clergyman, to promote legislation similar to that put forward in England. Attempts were made to introduce the Bill into different State legislatures but met with no success.

The English Bill applies only to those of twenty-one years of age, who are of sound mind, and who are suffering from a painful and incurable disease. An application has to be signed by the patient in the presence of two witnesses and submitted to the "Euthanasia Referee". This referee is a new official, whose appointment by the Minister of Health is provided for in the Bill. Two medical certificates are also required, one from the patient's doctor and the other from a specially qualified practitioner. The referee interviews the patient and establishes that he knows what he is doing, after which, euthanasia is administered by a licensed practitioner in the presence of an official witness. The American Bill is similar to the English one except that it omits the provision for the appointment of a referee. Application is to be made to the courts, which are then to appoint a committee of three competent persons "not opposed to euthanasia", two of whom must be doctors, to examine the applicant. They report to the courts whether the applicant understands the "nature and purpose" of the petition, and this must either be granted or denied within three days. Provision is made for an appeal if the petition is denied.

Under both Bills the machinery provided is intended to be a safeguard against abuse, but it has struck most people as being cumbrous and cold-blooded. Dr Glanville Williams, a supporter of euthanasia, has put forward an alternative proposal, providing a simple defence for a medical practitioner who administers euthanasia. The defence would lay down that no medical practitioner should be guilty of any act done intentionally to accelerate the death of a seriously ill patient, "unless it is proved that the act was not done in good faith with the consent of the patient and for the purpose of saving him from severe pain in an illness believed to be of an incurable and fatal character". Dr Williams' suggestion would achieve the same end as the Bills of the euthanasia societies but without their objectionable procedures. Discretion would be left to the individual doctor, as at present, but he would have the added protection, that if he killed a patient on request he would be protected by law.

Both these proposals would be unacceptable to the Christian conscience since they would constitute a direct attack by the law on the principle of the sanctity of life. In both cases the law would be authorizing the taking of innocent life, and thus be injuring the common good. General moral opinion in England and the United States is against compulsory euthanasia and has grave doubts about the legitimacy of voluntary euthanasia. Since the experience of Nazi Germany during the war the whole euthanasia movement has fallen into disrepute. Under these circumstances Christians are fully justified in opposing any attempt to introduce legalized euthanasia and can be reasonably confident that their efforts will be successful.

CHAPTER IV

BIRTH CONTROL

The traditional position of the Catholic Church has been to condemn contraception as sinful, and despite the changed views of other Churches it maintains its position today. The Catholic viewpoint on family planning has on the other hand modified, and has moved from a position of suspicion and mistrust to one of full acceptance in the conditions presented by the modern world. There has also been a shift in position in the advocacy of large families. In one sense this still remains the Catholic ideal, but Catholic writers are now more aware than ever in the past of the importance of taking into account prevailing social conditions when considering the question of the ideal size of the family. In advanced countries the expectation of a reasonable standard of life has to be taken into account: in countries which are struggling to emerge from grinding poverty, and which have to deal with an ever-increasing population which absorbs the fruits of economic advance as soon as they have been achieved, the ideal of a large family is clearly quite inappropriate.

Catholic condemnation of contraception goes back to the Fathers of the Church. St Augustine is quite clear that "intercourse even with one's legitimate wife is unlawful and wicked where the conception of the offspring is prevented. Onan, the son of Juda, did this, and the Lord killed him for it."[1] The Old Testament also contains the general exhortation to "in-

[1] *De adulterinis coniugiis*, II, 12.

crease and multiply", but this has to be read in the historical
context of its time and the tribal needs of the Jewish people.

Rejection of contraception is part of the natural law teaching on which so much Catholic ethical and philosophical teaching is founded. St Thomas Aquinas taught that contraception
was contrary to the natural law, and his teaching was re-stated
in modern times by Pius XI in his Encyclical on Christian
marriage, *Casti Connubii*: "Since therefore the conjugal act is
destined primarily by nature for the begetting of children,
those who in exercising it deliberately frustrate its natural
effect and purpose, sin against nature and commit a deed
which is shameful and intrinsically vicious." The natural law
tradition divides the purposes of marriage into two, the
primary purpose of marriage which is procreation, and the
secondary ends where are found lumped together such matters
as fostering the mutual love of the spouses and the reduction
of concupiscence. Man can distinguish these two sets of ends
by the use of his reason which reveals God's purpose in the
universe and God makes known his purpose by certain
"given" physical arrangements. These arrangements may not
be flouted at will.

Some Catholic theologians have found the Augustinian–
Thomist approach to marriage, with its emphasis on the
procreative purpose it serves and its underestimation of the
personal factors of friendship and love between the spouses,
unsatisfactory. The pioneer writers in this field were Dietrich
von Hildebrand and Herbert Doms, who wished to see stress
laid on the personal aspects of marriage and its rôle in increasing mutual love and therefore mutual perfection in the
spouses. Dr Doms rejects the idea of a purpose outside themselves for which the spouses marry. The purpose of marriage,
he writes in his book *The Meaning of Marriage*, "consists in
the constant, vital ordination of husband and wife to each
other until they become one. If this is so, there can no longer
be sufficient reason, from this standpoint, for speaking of
procreation as the primary purpose (in the sense in which

St Thomas used the phrase) and for dividing off the other purposes as secondary." The meaning of marriage is the community of life between the spouses, and of this the child is the fruit and visible embodiment. Dr Doms incurred an ecclesiastical censure for his book, and in 1944 the Holy Office reasserted the basic distinction between the primary and secondary ends of marriage.

Despite this the influence of Dr Doms and his followers has been profound. Their thought takes into account a whole range of psychological data of which scholastic theologians were unaware, and it is in accord with the contemporary, personal, approach to marriage. Pius XI himself was aware of this modern approach and states in his Encyclical *Casti Connubii*: "This mutual, interior moulding of husband and wife, this determined effort to perfect one another, can in a very real sense, as the Roman Catechism teaches, be said to be the chief reason and purpose of matrimony, provided matrimony be looked at not in the restricted sense as instituted for the proper conception and education of children, but more widely as a blending of life as a whole, and the mutual interchange and sharing thereof." The Pope of course retains the distinction between primary and secondary ends which Dr Doms rejects. It has been suggested that if this distinction is abandoned the whole basis for the condemnation of contraception falls to the ground, yet this is not the necessary result of placing the relational and conceptual ends of marriage on an equal basis. The intrinsic nature of *coitus* is the giving and receiving of seed, and without this neither its conceptual nor relational ends are achieved, hence the necessity to reject contraception. Intercourse with a contraceptive becomes an onanistic act ontologically distinct from true *coitus*.

Catholic apologists in the past have employed a variety of minor arguments to support their condemnation of contraception, but some of these lack supporting evidence, while in the case of others the argument loses much of its force through being equally applicable to the use of the safe period. Contraception is said to have harmful effects on the health of the woman and even to be a contributory cause of cancer. Sterility, it is alleged, is another by-product. Medical opinion can be produced to support these allegations, but the majority of doctors see no harm resulting to the woman's health from the use of contraceptives, provided they are employed correctly. The Biological and Medical Committee of the Royal Commission on Population denied that there was any evidence that contraceptive methods approved by the medical profession produced sterility.

A favoured Catholic argument used to be that contraceptives inevitably led to population decline and hence to a loss of power and influence for the nation that employed them. As has been noted, population decline in a poor country, far from being an evil, may be of positive benefit, in that it allows the standard of living of the population remaining to be raised. Population growth is a worldwide phenomenon, but it has been fastest in the underdeveloped countries of Asia, Africa and South America, precisely the areas least fitted to support an increased population. Cause of the swift growth in population—in Puerto Rico the annual increase, for example, is 3 per cent—is primarily the reduction of disease and a fall in the death rate. To quote from the Puerto Rican experience again, the death rate fell from 11·8 per thousand in 1947 to 7·2 in 1955. The scope for further reduction is shown if one compares the infant mortality rates in different countries. In Britain it is 26·5 but in India it is nearer 200.

Even in the advanced countries population is increasing. The United States has one of the highest rates of increase of population in the world, and both France and the United Kingdom are countries of increasing population. Yet the United States and the United Kingdom are the two countries where use of contraceptives is most widespread. Countries used to be thought to pass through a fourfold cycle in relation to births and deaths. First, both birth and death rates are high, and this is followed by a period of high birth rates and falling death rates. Then both birth and death rates fall, and finally the country passes into a period of low birth and death rates. A fifth stage must now be posited, when a country has reached a certain degree of affluence, the birth rate tends to go up again through the voluntary choice of parents who wish to have more children. This has certainly happened in the United States, and to a lesser but still marked extent in Britain.

The Catholic Church does not object to family planning and indeed is rapidly coming round to the position where this is enjoined as a positive duty on parents. The dispute between Catholics and non-Catholics over birth control has narrowed to one of means rather than of ends. The means approved by the Catholic Church is the rhythm method of birth control. For hundreds of years the existence of a sterile period in women has been a subject for speculation amongst doctors, but it was not until this century that reliable means have been developed to calculate its duration. Ogino of Japan and Knaus of Austria undertook the pioneer research work into the safe period, publishing their conclusions in 1930. Ovulation occurs only once during a woman's menstrual period of twenty-eight days and conception can only occur when the egg is present. Accordingly if the date of ovulation can be accurately calculated the point at which the sterile period begins can be ascertained. Research based on the findings of Ogino and Knaus shows that ovulation takes place on the fifteenth day before the onset of menstruation. With this basic piece of information the sterile period for the individual woman can be worked out taking into account her menstrual cycle which varies within constant limits of twenty-five to thirty days. Allowance has to be made for the period of the life of the ovum, one day, and for the time for which the male sperm can survive in the female genital tract, two days. If a woman's menstrual cycle is absolutely regular, then the period of fertility will be five days and the sterile period twenty-three days. Charts can be supplied to women by which after the necessary facts have been ascertained they can work out their own sterile and fertile periods for themselves.

Another method of fixing the date of ovulation is by use of a basal body temperature chart. This is founded on the fact that immediately after ovulation the normal temperature of a woman rises and remains at this level shortly before the next menstrual period. By combining this method with that described in the previous paragraph, the number of days on which intercourse must be restricted can be reduced. A third method of calculating ovulation takes into account the fact that in order to nourish the egg, the womb secretes sugar, and this sugar is present only at the time of ovulation. Chemically prepared tape is held against the womb which turns green if sugar is present. Four days' abstention after the tape turns green is recommended.

How satisfactory is the safe period as a method of birth control? Its chief advantage is that it allows a complete physiological union which is clearly not possible when a contraceptive is employed. On the other hand it does have undoubted disadvantages. An error can easily be made by the woman when she is using her chart. Apart from this, ovulation may take place on days other than the fifteenth or a woman's cycle may be so irregular that it is impossible to calculate her ovulation day with any accuracy. To some extent this difficulty has been overcome by the development of drugs that stabilize the menstrual period. A certain amount of research has been undertaken into the effectiveness of the rhythm method, but the results yielded are conflicting. Estimates have varied from a rate of ineffectiveness of 30 per cent to that of 3 per cent. It seems reasonable to assume that as yet the rhythm method is not as safe as certain means of appliance control.

Catholic theologians approve of the rhythm method of birth control on the ground that it is not unnatural, since it involves no interference with the "given" physical facts of nature, but merely takes advantage of them to achieve a certain end.

Nevertheless, it is generally agreed that there are conditions limiting the legitimacy of its use. Both parties to the marriage must give their free consent to its employment and they must be able to bear any strains which it may impose. Finally, there must be some serious reason for its employment. Among the factors to be considered are the number of children the parents already possess, their financial position, their housing situation, etc. Use of the rhythm method to exclude children entirely from the marriage would not be justified. In a statement of October 9th, 1951, to the Italian midwives, in which he gave express approval to the rhythm method, Pius XII added:

> The matrimonial contract which confers upon the parties the right to satisfy the inclination of nature, constitutes them in a state of life, the state of matrimony. Now upon the parties who make use of this right by the specific act of their state, nature and the creator impose the function of providing for the conservation of the human race.... It follows from this that to enter upon the state of matrimony, to make constant use of the faculty proper to it and only in matrimony allowable, and on the other hand consistently and deliberately, and without serious reason, to shirk the primary duty it imposes, would be to sin against the very meaning of married life.

Quite apart from the personal situation of the parties the general social and economic conditions of the country in which they live may be taken into consideration. The economic conditions in an underdeveloped country might well be a serious enough reason for resort to rhythm.

At one time the Catholic position on birth control was shared by the whole of Christendom, but the other Churches have gradually altered their position so that today apart from Catholics only the Orthodox condemn contraception. The Church of England has passed from a position of condemning contraceptives to one approving of their use. In 1920 the Lambeth Conference, which expresses the mind of the Anglican Communion, was unambiguous in its condemnation of contraception. "We utter an emphatic warning", declared the Con-

ference, "against the use of unnatural means for the avoidance
of conception, together with the grave dangers—physical,
moral and religious—thereby incurred, and against the evils
with which the extension of such use threatens the race. In
opposition to the teaching which, under the name of science
and religion, encourages married people in the deliberate
cultivation of sexual union as an end in itself, we steadfastly
uphold what must always be regarded as the governing considerations of Christian marriage. One is the primary purpose
for which marriage exists, namely the continuance of the race
through the gift and heritage of children; the other is the
paramount importance in married life of deliberate and
thoughtful self-control." The Conference followed up this
resolution with another calling for a campaign against the
sale of contraceptives. By 1930 the Conference had shifted its
position to allow of the use of contraceptives in limited circumstances. In 1958 the Conference passed a motion unani-
mously approving contraception.

The Conference believes that the responsibility for deciding
upon the number and frequency of children has been laid by
God upon the consciences of parents everywhere: that this
planning, in such ways as are mutually acceptable to husband
and wife in Christian conscience, is a right and important
factor in Christian family life and should be the result of
positive choice before God. Such responsible parenthood, built
on obedience to all the duties of marriage, requires a wise
stewardship of the resources and abilities of the family as well
as a thoughtful consideration of the varying population needs
and problems of society and the claims of future generations.

In 1934 the bishops of the Protestant Episcopal Church in
America had taken their cue from Lambeth and on
October 8th passed a resolution by 44 votes to 38, approving
"the efforts now being made to secure for licensed physicians,
hospitals and medical clinics, freedom to convey such information (on birth control) as is in accord with the highest
principles of eugenics and a more wholesome family life

wherein parenthood may be undertaken with due respect for the health of the mother and the welfare of the child". In April 1959 a study group appointed by the World Council of Churches met at Mansfield College, Oxford, to consider the problems raised by birth control and the increase in world population. The twenty-one members of the group represented the principal Churches represented on the World Council, and at the end of their investigations they published a report, "Responsible Parenthood and the Population Problem", approving of the use of contraceptives. Only the Orthodox representatives expressed their dissent.

One reason for the change in attitude of the Churches towards contraception is a revised assessment of the population problem. When the Lambeth Conference met in 1920 the problem appeared to be that of underpopulation and race decline. By 1958 the whole emphasis had shifted to the dangers of overpopulation, and countries with this problem such as India, the West Indies and African nations, were strongly represented at Lambeth. Theological changes had also prepared the way for the acceptance of contraception. The 1958 Conference declined to subordinate the companionate end of marriage to the end of reproduction. These ends, it held, cannot be separated in importance, "are not subordinated one to the other; they are not directly related to one another; their relationship, in the developing experience of Israel is to be found in yet a third area—that of the place of the family in giving responsible security to the children born of the love of husband and wife". Anglican theologians have also stressed the importance of *henosis* and the act of *coitus* in marriage. These theologians admit that procreation must not be totally excluded from marriage but insist that it is not the primary end of every act of *coitus*. In a sense the theologians are having the best of both worlds. They elevate and sanctify the act of *coitus* but at the same time they hold that what actually constitutes *coitus* is not something given by God but something that is variable at the will of the parties. Once this position is adopted it is impossible to stop short of the acceptance of any physical acts between a married couple, provided they honestly consider them to be lawful.

Other Protestant theologians refuse to accept the Catholic position on birth control since it limits human freedom. "The prohibition of birth control", said Reinhold Niebuhr in his Gifford lectures for 1939, "assumes that the sexual function in human life must be limited to its function in nature, that of procreation. But it is the very character of human life that all animal functions are touched by freedom and released into more complex relationships. This freedom is the basis of both creativity and sin." Joseph Fletcher has applied this general view in detail in his book *Morals and Medicine*:

> With the medical technology of contraception, parenthood and birth control become matters of moral responsibility, of intelligent choice. We are able to control our fertility. No longer do we have to choose between reproduction and continence. Sex is no longer a helpless submission to biological consequences. Nor is the only alternative a denial of sexual love either *in toto*, or according to lunar calculations in a sophisticated and doubtful rhythm mathematics. When such calculations enter in, the spontaneity of love goes out. Rhythm is a denial of freedom; it offers only an alternative of necessities, not a method of true control.

English law in the past has been influenced by the traditional Catholic and Christian viewpoint on the purpose of marriage and on the status of contraception. English judges in the nineteenth century were united in laying down procreation of children as the primary purpose of marriage. In 1946 the Court of Appeal held that for a husband to refuse to have intercourse without a contraceptive, against the wish of the wife, constituted grounds for the granting to her of a decree of nullity. Lord Justice du Parcq held "that sexual intercourse cannot be said to be complete where a husband deliberately discontinues the act of intercourse before it has reached its natural termination or when he artificially prevents the natural

termination which is the passage of the male seed into the
body of the woman. To hold otherwise would be to affirm that
a marriage is consummated by an act so performed that one
of the principal ends, if not the principal end, of marriage is
intentionally frustrated." Two years later in the case of *Baxter*
v. *Baxter* the House of Lords overruled the Court of Appeal
and refused a nullity decree to a husband under similar circumstances. "It is indisputable", said Lord Jowitt, "that the
institution of marriage generally is not necessary for the procreation of children; nor does it appear to be a principal end
of marriage as understood in Christendom. . . ."

The attitude of the law to contraceptives themselves has
undergone a revolutionary change. In the nineteenth century,
contraceptive information was classed as obscenity and their
sale doubtless came within the common law offence of publishing obscene matter. In 1877 a famous prosecution occurred
when Charles Bradlaugh and Annie Besant were prosecuted
for publishing Charles Knowlton's *Fruits of Philosophy*, a
pamphlet advocating birth control, which had been written by
a Massachusetts physician. The Bradlaugh case was the first
of a series of prosecutions of what may be described as "sex
manuals". The case really began in 1876 with the prosecution
of a Bristol bookseller for selling the book, which had in fact
been freely available in England for forty years. He pleaded
guilty. Charles Bradlaugh and Annie Besant, who had formed
the "Free Thought Publishing Company", decided to re-
publish the book in London without the illustrations which
may have prompted the original prosecution. They were both
arrested on a warrant and presented for trial at the Old Bailey
before Chief Justice Cockburn. The jury brought in a verdict
of guilty and both defendants were fined £200 and sentenced
to six months' imprisonment. Bradlaugh then moved for a
writ of error on the grounds that the indictment was bad for
setting out only the title and not the whole book. This point
was sustained by the High Court, who quashed the conviction
as well as the order which had been made for the destruction

of the pamphlets. The effects of the prosecution were extraordinary. Before 1876 the circulation of *Fruits of Philosophy*
had been only 1,000 per year, but by August 1881 no fewer
than 185,000 had been sold. The case is a good example of the
danger of prosecuting books for obscenity unless there is a
high degree of likelihood of success. Unsuccessful prosecutions serve only to advertise books and increase their sales.
Speaking of the prosecution of *Fruits of Philosophy*, Sir
Alexander Cockburn stated: "A more ill advised and more
injudicious prosecution never was instituted. Here is a work
which has been published for more than forty years and which
appears never to have got into general circulation and which
by these injudicious proceedings has got into large circulation
so that the sale has suddenly risen by thousands." After the
case, knowledge of contraceptive methods spread and the
work was carried forward by the Malthusian League, founded
in 1878 with Annie Besant as its secretary.

After the Bradlaugh–Besant case the law made no further
attempt to suppress contraceptive information which was *bona
fide* set out. In 1879 Annie Besant published her own treatise,
The Law of Population, which was an immediate success and
sold many thousands of copies. The book was never subjected
to prosecution in England. Despite the quiescence of the law,
non-legal opposition to contraception was still substantial. In
1887 Dr Henry Allbutt's name was erased from the medical
register by the General Medical Council for publishing a
handbook on birth control, *The Wife's Handbook*. It was not
until after the First World War that the social restrictions on
dissemination of birth control information ceased to operate.
Marie Stopes founded the "Society for Constructive Birth
Control", and in 1921 opened the first birth control clinic in
London. Her example was followed by others, so that contraception gradually won social acceptance.

Today in England the sale and use of contraceptives is
widespread. Books are no longer considered obscene if they
advocate or describe methods of birth control. "It cannot be

assumed", said the Home Secretary in answer to a question in the House of Commons in 1922, "that a court would hold a book to be obscene merely because it deals with the subject referred to." Sale of contraceptives is not restricted except where by-laws impose restriction on the sale from slot machines. The by-laws were suggested by the Home Secretary in a circular of October 22nd, 1949, after alarm had been expressed about the spread of slot machines and the consequent purchase of contraceptives by teenagers. The Home Secretary circulated a model by-law suggesting that it should be dealt with on a local level, since it was only a problem in some public places. Advertisements for contraceptives are not considered obscene provided their manner of presentation is not pornographic.

Where birth control is still subject to some restriction is under the National Health Service. Contraceptive advice may be given in maternal and child welfare clinics only to those married women for whom a pregnancy would be detrimental to health. Other married women must seek advice at the voluntary birth control clinics which are to be found in many areas. Local authorities may, if they obtain the approval of the Minister, open contraceptive clinics, and many clinics of the Family Planning Association are conducted on the premises of the local authority or regional hospital boards. Grants may be made by local authorities to voluntary organizations providing birth control advice. General practitioners in the service are free to give advice about contraceptives to their patients, but contraceptive appliances are not available on a National Health Service prescription. If a patient requires them on medical grounds and cannot afford to pay for them, then payment may be authorized by a local authority medical officer or a hospital consultant. These restrictions under the Health Service have been subject to widespread criticism. As early as April 1926 the House of Lords passed Lord Buckmaster's motion calling for the removal of restrictions on advice to married women. The Royal Commission on Population also suggested that the restrictions, as far as married women are concerned, should be removed. "Control by men and women over the numbers of their children", says the report, "is one of the first conditions of their own and the community's welfare, and in our view mechanical and chemical methods of contraception have to be accepted as part of the modern means, however imperfect, by which it can be exercised." The Report did not suggest the giving of advice to unmarried women, but this recommendation was made in the P.E.P. study *Population Policy in Great Britain*, published in 1948.

In the United States, the sale and distribution of contraceptives is in theory controlled by Federal law. To use the mails for the purpose of conveying contraceptives is a felony punishable by a fine of not more than five thousand dollars or five years' imprisonment both for a first offence, and double these penalties for a second offence. The statute covers books giving contraceptive information. Importing of contraceptives or use of a common carrier to transport them is also forbidden by Federal law. At first sight these statutes appear to impose the severest restrictions on the sale of contraceptives, but they have been made subject to a series of judicial interpretations which greatly limit their effect. In practice they are only applied if there is an intent on the part of the sender to use them for illegal or immoral purposes. Manufacturers of contraceptives are thus enabled to send them to doctors and druggists without fear of being prosecuted at law. Under the customs law, the import of obscene books is forbidden, but it has been held by the courts that a book on contraception is not in itself obscene. In 1931 a charge of obscenity was brought against a book by Marie Stopes entitled *Contraception*. Judge Woolsey said: "It is a scientific book written with obvious seriousness and with great decency, and it gives information to the medical profession regarding the operation of birth control clinics and the instruction necessary to be given at such clinics to women who resort thereto." Judge Woolsey held that it might be imported freely.

Apart from Federal law the sale of contraceptives and the giving of contraceptive information is governed by State law. Twenty American States have no legislation on the subject, but seventeen prohibit the trade in contraceptives with exemptions for doctors, chemists and others operating under special licence. Five States, Connecticut, Kansas, Massachusetts, Mississipi and Nebraska, forbid the sale or advertising of contraceptives. Prohibition of advertising of contraceptives is more widespread and is found in thirty States, although fifteen make exceptions for medical journals and textbooks. In a number of States sale of contraceptives from slot machines is penalized by law.

Like the Federal law, the State laws have been subject to so much liberalizing judicial interpretation that apart from the laws restricting advertising and sale from slot machines they are virtually without effect. In two States, however, the laws do have practical consequences, Connecticut and Massachusetts. The Connecticut statute provides that: "Any person who shall use any drug, medicinal article or instrument for the purpose of preventing conception, shall be fined not less than fifty dollars or imprisoned not less than sixty days nor more than one year or be both fined and imprisoned." In so far as the statute forbids the "use" of a contraceptive it is clearly not enforceable, but it has prevented the opening of birth control clinics in Connecticut. A number of clinics were opened in 1935 but these were raided in 1939 and after an adverse court decision in 1940 were closed down and have not subsequently been re-opened. The 1940 case, *State* v. *Nelson*, concerned two physicians and a nurse, who were indicted for advising a married woman to use a contraceptive. They contended that the statute was unconstitutional, unless it was interpreted to exempt the medical profession from its operation. The Supreme Court of Errors, by a vote of three to two, upheld the statute as being constitutional without any exception for doctors. In 1942 the courts went further and in *Tileston* v. *Ullman* held that the statute applied even where a doctor testified that pregnancy would entail a specific danger to health. The Supreme Court, again by a vote of three to two, held that abstention must have been considered by the legislature as an alternative to the use of contraceptives in such a situation.

In Massachusetts a statute dating from 1879 prohibits the publication of any printed matter containing birth control information and also the distribution of contraceptives. In *Commonwealth* v. *Allison*, a case of 1917, the statute was declared constitutional and a number of pamphlets giving birth control information were banned. In *Commonwealth* v. *Gardiner* in 1938, the courts rejected the argument that doctors were exempt from the statute when prescribing contraceptives for reasons of health. On the other hand, in 1940 it was held that distribution of prophylactics, intended to prevent the spread of venereal disease, was not illegal. As in Connecticut, there are no birth control clinics in Massachusetts.

In 1937 a special committee appointed by the American Medical Association stated that it had been unable to find any evidence that the existing laws on contraceptives had interfered with any medical advice which a physician had been called upon to supply to his patients. Their judgement is echoed by Judge Morris Ploscowe writing in the New York University *Law Review* in 1956. "I am not too concerned", he writes, "about this failure of Massachusetts and Connecticut to permit the dissemination of contraceptive information. The corner drugstore is always available for the purchase of prophylactic devices which are used mainly for contraceptive purposes. If more is desired, then the doctors in neighbouring States are available for consultation." The Planned Parenthood Leagues on the other hand strongly resent the existing laws in Connecticut and Massachusetts. They argue that they discriminate against the poor who cannot afford a private consultation with the doctor and that while allowing the sale of the less efficient contraceptives as prophylactics, they impose a ban on the more effective. Various attempts have been made to get these statutes declared unconstitutional but so far all have failed.

How extensive is the use of contraception in England and the United States? In England it appears to be widely practised amongst all classes of the community. The Family Planning Association operates hundreds of clinics and over a quarter of a million people visit them each year. The Royal Commission on Population estimated that while only 15 per cent of couples married before 1910 used birth control, for those married between 1940 and 1947 the proportion had risen to 55 per cent. The commission expected that the proportion would eventually rise to 70 per cent. In the United States it has been estimated that 90 per cent of fertile American women who have been married fifteen years or more practise some form of birth control.[2] This statistic includes the use of the safe period. Twenty-eight States have planned parenthood centres and apart from Connecticut and Massachusetts, nearly six hundred maternal health clinics and child-spacing information centres are found scattered throughout the country. The majority of medical schools in the United States provide their students with instruction in contraceptive techniques. In some States, birth control services are available through State or county maternal health clinics.

What should be the attitude of Catholics to laws prohibiting contraception? Does Catholic theology require Catholics to support and work for laws of this nature? The first point to be made is that one cannot conclude that because an act is contrary to natural law it should therefore be prohibited by positive law. To adopt such a standpoint is to obliterate the distinction between law and morals, the principles underlying which were explored in Chapter II. A breach of natural law must be a fit subject for legislation and injure the common

[2] See *Our Crowded Planet*, edited by Fairfield Osborn. London: 1963.

good substantially before it is forbidden by law. The law must be capable of enforcement and equitable in its incidence. Finally, if a law would cause greater evils than those it is intended to eradicate, recourse to legislation should be avoided.

In England so widespread is the practice of contraception, and it is now, however erroneously, thought to be morally justifiable, that any attempt by Catholics to secure a legislative ban would be doomed to failure. The Catholic population constitutes only a small proportion—probably about 10 per cent of the population—and it can only secure the passage of laws when it co-operates with other groups. The question is therefore largely an academic one, and English Catholics, although they have condemned contraception as contrary to the natural law and the teaching of the Church, have not in fact made any attempt to secure a legislative ban on contraceptives.

In the United States, as has been seen, the position is somewhat different. Catholics in Connecticut and Massachusetts have campaigned vigorously to keep the present laws on the statute books and so far have achieved success. Are these activities justified? The banning of the *use* of contraceptives by law in Connecticut hardly seems justifiable. To enforce such a law would involve a degree of interference with the life of the individual which would be quite intolerable. Private individuals and married couples would have to be subjected to a degree of supervision which is not found even in Communist police States. Banning the sale of contraceptives, on the other hand, is, *prima facie*, more reasonable, since a sale, being a public act, is more capable of regulation by law. However, such a law is only enforceable where it is supported by prevailing moral opinion. In a Catholic country such as Ireland, a public opinion is found which condemns contraception, and which forms a solid foundation on which the law can be built. In the United States, no such opinion exists, and a Catholic-supported ban on contraception is widely regarded as an unjustified interference with civil liberties. The laws of

Connecticut and Massachusetts are not in fact enforceable, and save for the exclusion of birth control clinics are without effect. Even on this particular point, the presence of clinics in neighbouring States does much to undo the effect of the ban. Catholics, then, in campaigning for such laws gain little for public morality. They do, however, increase the fear of Catholicism in the minds of non-Catholics and increase the likelihood that when Protestants visualize the Church, the image will not be that of a religious body but of a political power structure. This is a high price to pay for the main-tenance of ineffectual statutes.

The argument that contraception is contrary to the natural law is of little effect since the vast majority of non-Catholics are unable to see that this is so. The evil of birth control is not among that class of wrongs, such as murder, which are immediately apparent to the mass of mankind. For the pur-pose of civil legislation, then, Catholics would be well advised if they treated the morality of birth control as one within the sphere of moral theology, based on the acceptance of the teaching mission of the Church, rather than of natural ethics. Where a prohibitory law is impossible, a regulatory law may be desirable, and efforts to preserve public morality would be more effective if confined to those measures which command general support, such as the banning of the sale of contracep-tives from slot machines or the restriction of sale to adults.

While civil strife continues between Catholics and non-Catholics in the United States over contraception, the centre of gravity of the question has shifted from the domestic to the world scene. The problem of an ever-increasing world popu-lation is one of the most serious affecting mankind. It involves not only the physical welfare of millions of people facing a daily crisis of starvation and want, but raises a host of inter-related social questions, and ultimately the question of war and peace. In 1950 world population was 2,500 million: by 1958 it had reached 2,800 million: today it is 3,000 million, and is increasing at the rate of nearly fifty million a year.

Lord Boyd-Orr estimates that, if the present rate of increase continues, within eighty years the population of the world will have increased to 12,000 million.

How is this gigantic problem to be tackled? When the countries of the West faced their own population explosion in the last century, the industrial and agricultural revolutions were already under way, and enabled a greatly increased population to be supported. Apart from this, uncontrolled emigration to the New World provided the European countries with a safety valve. Today most of the increase in population is taking place in the underdeveloped countries of the world where industrialization has not taken place or where agriculture is organized on a primitive basis. These countries are desperately trying to raise their standard of living, but every increase in production is absorbed by the rise in numbers of the population. In India, for example, which has embarked on a series of five year plans, the population has increased by 25 per cent in ten years.

The spread of contraception is advocated by many as a solution to the world population problems, but there are grave difficulties in the way. In the first place, the countries of Asia and Africa are deeply suspicious of attempts by the West to limit their population. At an international conference held in Israel in 1960, representatives of many Afro-Asian States rejected birth control as a "trick of white men to keep down the black population". Secondly, contraception is not easily spread among primitive people who find the technique of using it difficult to master and in any case it is comparatively expensive. The development of a birth control pill has done something to render the spread of contraception easier, and in August 1963 the United States Federal Food and Drug Administration announced that the oral contraceptive "Enovid" is safe and effective when taken under doctor's orders. The recommendation was based on the report of a nine-man advisory committee of medical experts as well as on other information. "Enovid" was formerly recommended for use for a maximum period of two years: the new ruling authorizes its use for four. The agency pointed out that the pill could not be recommended for certain classes of patients, including women over thirty-five, because of possible hazards to health. Dr John Rock, a pioneer in the development of the oral contraceptive, in a book published in 1963, *The Time Has Come*, advocates the acceptance by the Catholic Church of the pill as a legitimate means of birth control. A suggestion has been made that such pills would be acceptable to Catholics as they leave the physical nature of the sexual act unimpaired. Catholic moralists, on the other hand, who have so far spoken or written on the subject, have been unanimous in condemning the use of the pills as a violation of divine law, since they prevent the natural end of the sexual act, procreation. A third reason for rejecting contraception as a solution to the world population problem is that whatever its effect in the long term, it cannot be adopted quickly enough to stem the minimum increase of one billion which is likely to be achieved by 1980.

The obvious agency for tackling the world population problem is the United Nations Organization and its subsidiary organizations such as the World Health Organization. Advocates of contraception have been persistent in their efforts to get the United Nations to sponsor their policies, but up to now have failed to achieve success. Catholic countries have been the principal opponents of the United Nations taking up a contraceptive programme, and they have been backed in this by countries of the Communist world. In 1952, the World Health Organization dropped a Norwegian proposal to study contraception as part of its official programme after opposition from Catholic delegates. Support for contraception in the United Nations has steadily increased—the latest vote resulted in a deadlock with equal numbers voting for and against—but there is still no majority for contraceptive policies. Catholic countries are certainly within their rights in opposing these: the United Nations is not a super-State but an agency for promoting co-operation between constituent members. Where there are irreconcilable differences of opinion the only possible policy is neutrality. If on the other hand the United Nations was to confine its sponsoring of family planning programmes to the rhythm method, Catholic objections would cease. Experiments were in fact carried out along these lines between 1952 and 1954 with help from the United Nations but were not a notable success. Two centres were selected in India, Lodi colony, an urban middle class centre, and Ramangaram, a rural town in Mysore. Three-quarters of the married couples in the selected centres expressed a desire to learn about family planning but only 13·6 per cent of the couples in Ramangaram and 28·3 per cent of those in Lodi colony were able to master the rhythm method. By March 1954 only 5 per cent and 7·5 per cent, respectively, were known to be following the method regularly.

India has in fact provided for her own programme of contraception and sterilization. Proposals to this effect were included in the first two five year plans, and the third five year plan provided 52 million dollars for family planning. In 1956 India had 147 birth control clinics, but by 1963 these had increased to 3,000. Distribution of contraceptives, most of them free, increased six times between 1956 and 1958. Sterilization has also been increasing. In many Indian States, hospitals are allowed to perform sterilizations, provided the applicant has already had three children. Sterilizations, which numbered 7,823 in 1956, had increased to 41,091 by 1960. Japan set out to reduce her birth rate using abortion as the principal instrument. A law of 1948 legalized abortion for medico-social reasons, and reduced the number of live births from 2,679,000 in 1947, to 1,563,000 ten years later, over 70 per cent of the reduction being due to abortion. The effect on women's health was grave and Japan has now shifted the emphasis from controlling population by abortion to contraceptive methods.

Catholics reject the policy of reducing world population by the employment of contraceptive methods not only as being contrary to the natural law but as a facile avoidance of the true solution to the problem. "What an error it would be", said Pius XII in his Christmas message of 1952, "to blame the natural law for the present miseries of the world when it is clear that these derive from the lack of mutual solidarity of men and peoples." What is needed is a concerted international effort to raise the living standards of the underdeveloped parts of the world. To achieve this end Lord Boyd-Orr has advocated the setting up of an international fund to provide for the industrial goods needed by these countries for the rapid increase of their food production. He calculates that it would take about 12,000 million dollars a year to provide sufficient food for all people within about ten years. This looks an astronomic figure until it is remembered that it is only 10 per cent of what the world is spending on military budgets. "It is the duty of Christians", writes the Protestant theologian Karl Barth, "(a) to support policies which involve sacrifice by the developed countries on behalf of the undeveloped ones, and (b) to advocate policies designed to increase the mobility of capital and labour between the developed and underdeveloped parts of the world."

This second solution of relaxation of the immigration laws has long been advocated by the Catholic Church. In a letter to the American bishops, dated December 24th, 1948, Pius XII said: "If, then, in some locality, the land offers the possibility of supporting a large number of people, the sovereignty of the State, although it must be respected, cannot be exaggerated to the point that access to this land is, for inadequate or unjustified reasons, denied to needy and decent people from other nations, whenever this does not hinder the public welfare as measured on honest-weight scales." The difficulty is that immigration of its nature can only be a supplementary solution to the world population problem. In the conditions of the modern world, the sort of migration that took place in the nineteenth century is not possible because of the disrupting effect it would have on the economy and social structure of the receiving countries.

The challenge presented to the Western world by the increase in population in the underdeveloped countries is immense. Nothing is more certain than that if the world becomes permanently divided between "have" and "have not" nations, the situation will be exploited by Communists, either Russian or Chinese, to facilitate the spread of their doctrines. Catholics, who have set their faces against contraception as a means of solving the world population problem, are under a positive duty to promote, by every means in their power, international co-operation so that the rich countries of the West can help those which are poor, and whose peoples are perpetually treading on the border of starvation and want.

CHAPTER V

ARTIFICIAL HUMAN

INSEMINATION

Artificial human insemination takes place when a woman is fertilized by means which are a substitution for natural intercourse. By the use of instruments semen is deposited in a woman's vagina, cervical canal, or uterus. When the semen employed comes from the husband the operation is known as *homologous* (A.I.H.): when it comes from a third party donor it is called *heterologous* (A.I.D.).

The morality of A.I.H. has been the subject of lively debate among Catholic theologians. Since these theologians have for so long stressed that procreation is the primary purpose of marriage, it might be thought that A.I.H. would have won majority approval, but this is not so. Difficulties have arisen over the method of obtaining the semen and also over the absence of any actual act of *coitus*. Catholic theologians are united in condemning A.I.H. when masturbation has been used as a means of obtaining the semen. The Catholic view is that masturbation is intrinsically wrong and its use cannot be justified even by the presence of a good motive such as the desire to have a child in a marriage which is proving sterile. This view is not shared by the Anglican theologians appointed by the Archbishop of Canterbury to consider artificial insemination in 1945, who issued their report in 1948. They concluded that although masturbation under normal circum-

stances would be sinful, considered in the special context of
A.I.H. it would not be so: "The act which produces the
seminal fluid, being in this instance directed towards the com-
pletion (impossible without it) of the procreative end of the
marriage, loses its character of self-abuse. It cannot in this
view be the will of God that a husband and wife should remain childless merely because an act of this kind is required
to promote conception."

Masturbation apart, semen may be obtained by aspiration
of spermatozoa by puncturing a testicle and the epididymis,
or by rectal massage of the prostate gland and seminal
vesicles with pressure on the ampulla of the vas deferens.
Some Catholic theologians, notably Fr Vermeersch and more
recently Fr Gerald Kelly of the U.S.A.,[1] have argued that
since these methods do not in any way arouse the venereal
appetite, and are employed to further the primary end of
marriage, their use is moral. The puncture of the epididymis,
writes Fr Kelly, "involves no use of the sexual *processes*,
hence cannot be properly styled an abuse, an unnatural sexual
act. Of itself, its intrinsic morality might partake of the nature
of a minor mutilation, somewhat similar to that involved in a
blood transfusion. Moreover, if extraction of seminal fluid
from the epididymis were absolutely wrong (like pollution
and onanism) it could never be allowed and physicians could
not resort to it even for examination purposes." Fr Kelly
argues that just as the individual in regard to his own self-
preservation may use abnormal means of nourishment to preserve his life, so married people, unable to have children by
means of normal sexual intercourse, are entitled to use abnormal means, provided those means are not sinful. Other
theologians have argued that to remove the male semen from
the generative organs is wrong because it destroys the ordination of the semen to generation required by the natural order.
The semen has to remain within the generative organs of

[1] *Medico-Moral Problems*; see Select Bibliography.

either male or female. Moreover, generation must be brought about by an act of natural conjugal intercourse.

This point was taken up by the Catholic committee on artificial insemination, appointed by Cardinal Godfrey to give evidence before the British government's departmental committee on artificial insemination, and whose evidence was published in the *Dublin Review* for spring 1960.[2]

> Read as a whole the design of the procreative function points to the moral obligation of achieving its purpose only by means of the conjugal act naturally performed. The parents of the human child are not mere agents in a biological process. They are persons, co-operating in the production of another person by a means which in nature's plan is hardly less important than the end itself. According to that plan, it is not enough that a child be the product of biological elements derived from its parents; it should be the fruit of an intimate physical act of personal union, prompted and inspired by mutual love. By this means husband and wife act in accordance with their nature which is spiritual as well as corporeal, they respect each other's personal dignity, and they establish that intimate personal relationship which conduces best to the security and harmonious development of their child. To divorce the biological act from the intimacy of the conjugal act is to do violence to human nature and to thwart the full and proper achievement of its purpose.

In reaching this conclusion the committee was clearly influenced by three statements of Pius XII in 1949, 1951 and 1956, in which he condemned artificial insemination as such. In his address of May 19th, 1956, to the Second World Congress on Fertility and Sterility, he made his own views clear beyond any shadow of doubt.

> Artificial insemination is beyond the right which husband and wife acquire by the contract of marriage, that is, the right to a full exercise of their natural sexual activity in the natural fulfilment of the marriage act. The marriage contract does not

[2] The government committee was presided over by Lord Feversham.

give them a right to artificial insemination. Such a right is in no way contained in the right to the natural marriage act, and can in no way be derived from it. Still less can one derive it from a right to "children"—as the first "end" of marriage. The marriage contract does not give this right, for it has as its object not "children" as such, but "natural acts" which are capable of and designed for the begetting of children. One must then say that artificial insemination violates the natural law and is immoral.

Two other means of obtaining semen are condemned by Catholic theologians, *coitus interruptus* and condomistic intercourse. No Catholic theologian can be found to defend *coitus interruptus*, but a minority have defended condomistic intercourse on the grounds that there is an actual functioning of the organs in conjugal sexual union and an intention to complete the act at a later stage. The majority, however, reject this view, holding that there is only an appearance of *coitus*, the essence of which is ejaculation of semen into the vagina, the orgasm itself in condomistic intercourse taking place outside of *coitus*.

There remains only "assisted" insemination, which is brought about after the act of *coitus* has taken place, either by aspiration of the semen by using a syringe or else by employing a tassette. Pius XII expressly excluded from his condemnation "the use of certain artificial means designed only to facilitate the natural act or to enable that act, performed in a natural manner, to attain its end". No theological difficulty arises from the use of these procedures as the full act of *coitus* has preceded them, and they are therefore considered legitimate by theologians.

Should A.I.H. be forbidden by law? The departmental committee appointed by the British government under the chairmanship of Lord Feversham, which reported in July 1960, concluded that it was rarely resorted to in Britain and should not be subject to legislation. It was estimated in 1955 that in the United States, 1,000 to 1,200 babies are conceived by artificial insemination each year, compared with approximately 4,000,000 children normally conceived. (Lang, *Artificial Insemination—Legitimate or Illegitimate*, McCalls, May 1955, p. 60.) Statutes directly dealing with A.I.D. have been proposed in a number of States, but none directly on the point has been enacted. On Christian principles there is no case for legal intervention. A.I.H., whatever one's views may be on its morality, in no way harms the common good, nor does it raise difficult social or legal problems. Whether it is employed or not should be left to the consciences of the husband and wife concerned, who will doubtless take into account the moral teaching of their religion on the subject. Any attempt to legislate on the subject would involve an interference with the private life of husband and wife which would be quite intolerable. An evil would be created worse than the evil intended to be avoided, and under these circumstances the matter is best left unregulated by law.

Unlike A.I.H., A.I.D. raises a great number of moral, social and legal problems. Catholic theologians are united in treating A.I.D. as intrinsically immoral. Artificial insemination outside of marriage is condemned without qualification, since both natural and divine law lay down that it is only within the marriage bond that children should be conceived. "Every use of the faculty given by God for the procreation of new life", states Pius XI in his Encyclical *Casti Connubii*, "is the right and privilege of the married state alone, by the law of God and of nature, and must be confined absolutely within the sacred limits of that state." Once this principle is accepted, the argument that every woman has the right to bear a child appears as purely sentimental. Those who put it forward concern themselves exclusively with the position of the mother and give no consideration to that of the child, yet such a child is placed in an anomalous social position and the absence of any father may lead to the development of neurosis and psychological disorder.

Within the marriage bond the use of A.I.D. is also condemned, on the ground that the marriage contract confers an exclusive right on the parties to the use of each other's reproductive and sexual functions, which cannot be waived. "Husband and wife", declared Pius XII in 1949, "alone have a reciprocal right over each other's body for the begetting of a child. This right is exclusive and inalienable, and cannot be ceded to another. Indeed it must be so out of consideration for the child. Nature lays upon those who give life to a child the responsibility for its care and upbringing. But between the husband of the marriage and the child born from a donor's seed (even with the husband's consent) there is no bond of descent, nor the moral and legal bonds which exist when the child is begot by husband and wife in marriage." Similar reasoning was used by the Archbishop of Canterbury's Commission to condemn A.I.D. in their 1948 report. "The husband", states the Report, "may not demand that his wife receive the seed of another man; nor may the wife demand that her husband authorize the reception of alien seed. By their mutual surrender to each other in the marriage contract, they set up an exclusive union and an exclusive mutual right. Neither has the power to introduce into that union any third party by such means as involve breach of that mutual right." Leading spokesmen of the Lutheran and Methodist Churches have also condemned A.I.D.

The Christian moral position on A.I.D. is accordingly clear. What is the status of A.I.D. at law? In this sphere there is considerable confusion. A.I.D., under English law, does not appear to be a crime. The common law is silent on the subject and no statute has been passed dealing with the matter. In the United States the position is similar, but there is just a possibility that by equating A.I.D. with adultery it might be brought within the sphere of the criminal law. Adultery is not a crime under English law, but in America many States have statutes which make it a criminal offence. In practice these do not seem to be enforced, but this policy could be changed in order to introduce a legislative ban on

A.I.D. A difficulty would be that American courts have held that to establish adultery at criminal law there must be an actual contact of sexual organs and some form of penetration of the female organ by that of the male.

A second perplexing legal problem is whether A.I.D. amounts to adultery at civil law, thus giving a ground for a divorce, or in certain jurisdictions for a decree of judicial separation. The early definitions of adultery do not give much guidance since they were framed before A.I.D. was thought of, but it is of some importance that in all cases before 1921 an element of carnal intercourse was required. In that year, in the Canadian case of *Orford* v. *Orford*, the judge stated that this was not required and that on grounds of public policy the courts should declare A.I.D. to constitute adultery. "The essence of the offence of adultery", said Judge Orde, "consists not in the moral turpitude of the act of sexual intercourse, but in the voluntary surrender to another person of the reproductive powers or faculties of the guilty person; and any submission of those powers or faculties to the service or enjoyment of any person other than the husband or wife comes within the definition of 'adultery'." In 1954, a similar view was taken by the judge in the United States case of *Doornbos* v. *Doornbos*, an Illinois decision. In this connection the decision of the House of Lords in the case of *Russell* v. *Russell* (1924) is relevant. Mrs Russell was fecundated *ab extra* by a third party and it was denied by counsel on her behalf that this constituted adultery. The House of Lords held otherwise. "The appellant conceived and had a child without penetration having been effected by any man", stated Lord Dunedin, "she was fecundated *ab extra*. . . . The jury came to the conclusion that she had been fecundated *ab extra* by another man unknown, and fecundation *ab extra* is, I doubt not, adultery."

A contrary view was taken in a more recent case, decided in Scotland in 1958, *Maclennan* v. *Maclennan*. Lord Wheatley, the judge, stated that normally when an act of sexual intercourse took place, a surrender was made of both the sexual and reproductive organs, but this was not necessary in all cases. Contraceptives might be employed or the woman might have had her reproductive organs removed or they might have ceased to function through natural causes. In such cases the conjunction of the sexual organs involving some degree of penetration would constitute adultery. Accordingly he concluded that impregnation as such could not constitute adultery. The test of adultery was sexual intercourse or carnal connection and for it to be committed the two parties must be physically present and engage in the sexual act at the same time. A.I.D., in Lord Wheatley's view, did not constitute adultery.

On the whole Lord Wheatley's view is to be preferred to its opposite, as being more in accord with past cases and with common sense. Rather than strain the definition of adultery so as to include A.I.D. it is better to treat it as a separate issue. The Royal Commission on Marriage and Divorce did so in its report of 1956 and recommended that it should be a separate ground for dissolution of marriage. This, of course, would only apply if A.I.D. had been carried out without the husband's consent, since consent would constitute a barrier of connivance to a divorce decree.

A third legal problem concerns the status of an A.I.D. child born of a married woman. Is it legitimate or illegitimate? The answer to this question is clearly of the greatest importance to the child, since on it will depend rights of succession to property, maintenance, and a host of allied matters. The weight of legal and medical opinion seems to be in favour of the child's illegitimacy. "The fact that conception is effected not by adultery or fornication", states an editorial in the *American Medical Association Journal* for May 6th, 1939, "but by a method not involving sexual intercourse, does not in principle seem to alter the concept of legitimacy. This concept seems to demand that the child be the actual offspring of the husband of the mother of the child. . . . If the semen of some other male is utilized the resulting child would seem to be illegitimate. The fact that the husband has freely consented to the artificial insemination does not have a bearing on the question of the child's legitimacy. If it did, by similar reasoning it might be urged that the fact that a husband had consented to the commission of adultery by his wife would legitimatize the issue resulting from the adulterous connection." In the House of Commons in 1945, Mr Henry Willink, then Minister of Health, maintained that an A.I.D. child was illegitimate. The same conclusion was reached by a subcommittee of the Michigan State Bar Association, which reported on A.I.D. in April 1956. There are few cases on the point and these are contradictory. In *Strnad* v. *Strnad*, a New York case of 1948, the judge held that the child would be legitimate if the husband gave his consent. In his view the case was similar to that of a child born out of wedlock, legitimated by the subsequent marriage of the parents. In *Doornbos* v. *Doornbos*, a case already referred to, A.I.D. children were held to be illegitimate. Whatever the view of the law, illegitimacy would be hard to establish in practice. Secrecy shrouds A.I.D. and the law presumes that a child born in lawful wedlock is a child of the marriage. The presumption of legitimacy is one of the strongest in both English and American law and can only be overcome by the clearest contrary evidence.

What, in the Christian view, should be the attitude of the law to A.I.D.? The Archbishop of Canterbury's Commission recommended that A.I.D. without the husband's consent should be an additional ground for divorce. Strictly speaking this is not a matter on which either Catholic or Anglican views are relevant, since the power of the State to dissolve a valid marriage is not recognized by either communion. Cardinal Godfrey's committee refrained from expressing any view on the question of divorce but did recommend that A.I.D. should be made a ground for judicial separation, unless the husband had consented to or condoned the insemination. It also suggested that where the husband had not consented to the operation he should be entitled to claim damages and costs against the donor and the inseminator.

The next legal question at issue is whether A.I.D. should be made a crime. The answer to this depends in part on the extent to which A.I.D. is practised and the likelihood of its spreading, but owing to the secrecy which surrounds it, reliable figures are very difficult to get. Few doctors appear to engage in this practice and it seems to be confined to a small group of specialists. Clinics concerned with the cure of sterility have made use of A.I.D., but its employment appears to be exceptional. At one clinic, founded by the Exeter and District Women's Welfare Association, one-seventh of the husbands who came for consultation were found to be sterile. Of these fewer than a quarter asked for A.I.D., and pregnancy occurred in only 50 per cent of the wives. Up to 1948 A.I.D. had been used in only 1 per cent of the cases in which advice had been sought because of involuntary sterility. Dr Margaret Jackson, one of the doctors specializing in A.I.D., reported to the Archbishop of Canterbury's committee that she had used A.I.D. in 34 cases, of which 17 were successfully inseminated. She also informed the committee that she had a panel of some twenty donors, one of whom had fathered seven children. In the House of Lords debate on the subject in February 1958, Lord Blackford stated that 7,000 A.I.D. births had taken place in the United Kingdom over the past twenty years. This figure was not accepted by the Feversham Committee, which concluded that the number of A.I.D. children in Britain was not likely to be more than 1,150 and that the annual birth rate of such children was in the region of 100 per year. The British Medical Association informed the Committee that the number of practitioners known to be regularly in the practice of A.I.D. was less than twenty, but even this figure was thought by the Committee to be an overestimation. The Committee itself received evidence from twelve doctors who had practised A.I.D., but of these five had ceased to do so. One concludes therefore that A.I.D. is at the moment practised in England on a very small scale, although the practice is spreading.

In the United States A.I.D. is more widely resorted to than in the United Kingdom. Eight American doctors gave evidence to the Feversham Committee that they had been responsible for over a thousand pregnancies up to 1959. Estimates of A.I.D. births have varied from 20,000, a figure given by Judge Ploscowe in 1951, to 50,000 by the *New York Post* in 1955. The Feversham Committee concluded that only 10,000 A.I.D. births had taken place in the U.S.A. by 1960. America has two sperm banks, one in Iowa and the other in New York.

The incidence of A.I.D. although small is far from negligible, and the figures for A.I.D. births, incomplete as they are, make out a *prima facie* case for dealing with it by law. The Feversham Committee concluded that A.I.D. should not be made a criminal offence, but both the Catholic Committee and the Archbishop of Canterbury's Commission recommended that it should. When the Feversham Committee was appointed in 1958, the Archbishop of Canterbury appointed a second committee to make recommendations, and this in contrast to its predecessor concluded that while A.I.D. should be considered unlawful it should not be made a specific criminal offence.

One reason for banning A.I.D. by law is the fraud and perjury to which it gives rise. On the birth of a child, the name of the father has to be given for purposes of registration, but because of the secrecy which is considered essential for the welfare of the child, this will not be the name of the donor but that of the wife's husband. Such false registration is an offence under section 4 of the Perjury Act of 1911 for which a sentence of seven years' imprisonment may be imposed, as well as a fine. An A.I.D. child may inherit property or titles to which in fact it has no right. Should the practice spread the possibility of marriage between half-brothers and half-sisters would be a real one, since the potential offspring of one donor can be measured in hundreds and even in thousands. These objections could be overcome by the provision of a compulsory register of A.I.D. births, giving a number for the donor's name, but this would do away with secrecy and there would be no means of guaranteeing that the register would be honestly used.

These points have their importance but the real objection to A.I.D. from the Christian point of view is a more fundamental one. Western society is based on the principle of monogamous marriage and on the institution of the family. A.I.D. subverts the family by substituting a different pattern of relationships for that which exists within the family between parents and children. It does not as its advocates claim create a family but merely the appearance of one. Thus A.I.D. constitutes a direct attack on the common good which justifies the intervention of the law. Furthermore, the abandonment of the principle that child bearing is only lawful with the co-operation of the parties to the marriage contract would open the way to the bearing of children by unmarried women utilizing the methods of A.I.D., thus constituting a further threat to the integrity of the family.

It has been argued that because A.I.D. is only practised by a tiny minority the intervention of the law is unnecessary, but the law must look not only to the present but the future. The danger of the practice spreading is a real one and a legislative ban might well prevent A.I.D. from becoming more widely used. The Feversham Committee, on the other hand, doubted whether a ban on A.I.D. would be enforceable in practice. The Committee considered that while prohibition of A.I.D. might deter some from engaging in it, it would not deter others, and their activities would be impossible to detect. A further point made by the Committee was that it might if banned fall into unscrupulous hands and increased scope be given to blackmail. The Catholic Committee recognized the force of this argument and suggested that if a legislative ban was considered impracticable then the law should at least refrain from giving any positive support or favour to A.I.D. and its practitioners. It further recommended that the maintaining of a bank of donors and the sale of semen be made illegal.[3]

To a very great extent the effectiveness of any law would depend on the co-operation of the medical profession. Some doctors would doubtless ignore it, but there is no reason to think that the vast majority would be prepared to defy the law. The Feversham Committee concluded that A.I.D. does not have the general support of the profession. Amongst those condemning the practice were committees of the Royal College of Physicians, the Royal College of Surgeons, Edinburgh, and the Royal College of Obstetricians and Gynaecologists. The Council of the British Medical Association stated that a "substantial body of opinion in the profession" regarded the practice as undesirable, although in the view of the Council it did not "contravene any of the accepted principles of scientific medicine". Since no country in the world has yet passed legislation dealing with artificial human insemination no evidence is available of the working of such laws in practice. It would seem, however, to be a reasonable conclusion that a prohibitory law would be far from being totally ineffective and would be influential in stopping the spread of A.I.D.

[3] In the U.S.A., New York doctors received the following circular during 1947. "We offer semen drawn from healthy and investigated professional donors. Suitable types for your patients' specifications. Active specimens guaranteed and delivered daily. Confidential service —office hours 5.30–7.30 p.m." The author of the circular was a young science graduate. The New York legislature replied by forbidding such activities under its sanitary code. This code lays down strict conditions to govern the providing of seminal fluid for artificial insemination. It also requires the doctor performing an artificial insemination to keep a record showing his own name, the name and address of the donor, the name and address of the recipient, the results of various prescribed examinations including tests for the Rh factor, and the date of the artificial insemination. The record is to be treated as confidential.

CHAPTER VI

STERILIZATION

Sterilization of human beings may be defined as an operation which deprives them of the capacity for reproduction. In veterinary surgery this result is obtained by castration, the surgical removal of the sexual organs, but this is not nowadays employed where human beings are concerned. The normal surgical operation for male sterilization is vasectomy and for women salpingectomy. Vasectomy is a simple operation which by ligating and resecting a small portion of the vas deferens stops the passage of spermatozoa into the seminal fluid and so renders it sterile. The operation was at one time thought to be irreversible but recent reports from India indicate that in many cases this can be brought about. One Indian worker in this field has recorded that out of twenty attempts to reverse vasectomy over a period of eight years, seventeen were successful. Sexual intercourse is not precluded by vasectomy. Salpingectomy cuts or ties the Fallopian tubes in a woman, so preventing the *ovum* from passing to the womb. This method is not infallible and a failure rate of between one and two per cent is estimated. Unlike vasectomy, salpingectomy is irreversible although attempts are now being made to develop a technique of re-uniting or re-implanting the severed tube. Other means of sterilizing women are hysterectomy (the removal of the womb) and oophorectomy (excision of the ovaries), both of which are of course irreversible.

Sterilization may be resorted to for a number of different

purposes. The most common is therapeutic sterilization. where a woman is sterilized because it is thought further pregnancies would prove dangerous. Sterilization may also be employed as a means of contraception where a couple wishes to avoid having children. Eugenic sterilization is designed to bring about racial improvement by preventing the transmission of physical or mental defect to future generations. Sterilization has also been used as a punishment for sexual offenders. Lastly, indirect sterilization should be noted. where the sterilization is not intended. but results from an operation carried out to preserve life or health.

The development of sterilization has been closely connected with eugenics, a science founded by Sir Francis Galton in the second half of the nineteenth century to study the influences that improve the inborn qualities of a race and those which develop them to the greatest advantage. Techniques of sterilization were perfected in the United States where vasectomy was developed by Harry C. Sharpe of the Indiana State Reformatory. At different times in the United States thirty-three States have had sterilization statutes in force. The most extensive use of sterilization was in Nazi Germany, where a statute was passed in 1933, the foundation of a plan to carry out 400,000 sterilizations made up of 200,000 feeble-minded, 80,000 schizophrenics, 60,000 epileptics, 20,000 insane manic depressives, 20,000 physically deformed, 18,000 deaf mutes, 10,000 chronic alcoholics, 6,000 sufferers from St Vitus's dance, and 4,000 blind. In the first year of the statute's operation 56,244 sterilizations were ordered.

The Nazi atrocities effectively discredited the use of sterilization for eugenic purposes, and in recent years its use has been chiefly advocated as a means of population control. In India voluntary sterilization has been actively encouraged by the government as part of its campaign to reduce the increase of population. State governments undertake their own campaigns, and some of them provide financial inducements to those who consent to be sterilized or persuade others to submit to the operation. It is difficult to assess the effects of this campaign, since the figures provided are inadequate. On March 28th, 1961, the *Daily Telegraph* reported that since the launching of the sterilization campaign in 1956, only 115,000 men and women had been operated on. The annual rate of sterilization for 1960 was reported in *The Guardian* for June 28th, 1961, as 38,000. Higher figures have come from the All India Family Planning Conference, where in early 1961 it was stated that 14,000 male sterilizations had been performed in the former State of Bombay in six weeks. In practice sterilization does not seem to have had much effect in solving India's population problem since the number of sterilizations carried out have been comparatively speaking few. In any case the majority of applicants come from the middle and upper classes and not from the poorer sections of the community where the birth rate is highest. Its employment in Puerto Rico amongst women seems to have been equally ineffective since most sterilizations there occur after the fourth pregnancy and some 29 per cent after the seventh.

In England sterilization is not often resorted to and interest in the subject seems to have declined since the 'thirties when it was much canvassed. In June 1932 a government committee was appointed "to examine and report on the information already available regarding the hereditary transmission and other causes of mental disorder and deficiency: to consider the value of sterilization as a preventive measure, having regard to its physical, psychological and social effects and to the experience of legislation in other countries permitting it: and to suggest what further enquiries might usefully be undertaken in this connection". In 1934 the committee, known from its chairman as the Brock Committee, presented its report, and recommended the legalizing by statute of voluntary sterilization. This recommendation has not been acted upon.

How effective is eugenic sterilization and how genuine is its social need? Those who advocate compulsory eugenic sterilization are not inhibited by any consideration of human rights.

"I think", wrote Justice Holmes, who was a life-long advocate of sterilization, "that the sacredness of human life is a purely municipal idea of no validity outside the jurisdiction. I believe that force mitigated so far as may be by good manners is the ultimate ratio." Dr Glanville Williams, another upholder of sterilization, notes with regret the striking contrast "between human fecklessness in our own reproduction and the careful scientific improvement of other forms of life under man's control. No rose-grower, pigeon-fancier or cattle breeder would behave as men do in their own breeding habits."

The benefits alleged to flow from compulsory sterilization are racial improvements which will hold in check the dangerous advance of insanity, feeble-mindedness, sexual perversion and criminality. These it is claimed are all inheritable and on the increase since defectives propagate at a higher rate than normal people. In fact there is no evidence that insanity and mental defect are on the increase. It is true that the number in mental homes and hospitals has grown in recent years, but this is the result of a more accurate diagnosis of mental disease, and the fact that many who before needed mental treatment and could not obtain it now find facilities within their reach. There is equally little basis to the conventional statement that defectives breed faster than normal people. "The supposed abnormal fertility of defectives", concluded the Brock Committee, "is, in our view, largely mythical and results from the accident that from time to time distressing exceptions to the general rule find their way into the Courts and are noticed in the press." Mental defectives in fact have a higher death rate and a lower birth rate than normal people as well as reduced sexual drives. Children of defectives have less chance of survival than those of normal parents. The Brock report records an investigation into 3,733 cases where the mother was defective in 3,247 and the father in 486. The marriages produced 8,841 children and of these 22·5 per cent died before reaching the age of seven.

A further assumption of those who support sterilization,

namely that mental defect and criminality are hereditary, is also open to question. No satisfactory biological theory of criminality has ever been developed, and the work of Lombroso, who claimed to have discovered a significantly higher proportion of vestigial and atavistic characters among criminals than among normal people, is now generally agreed to lack an adequate scientific basis. "Most writers agree", concluded the sterilization committee of the American Neurological Association in 1936, "that while there may be a constitution which in its reaction to the milieu appears as criminal conduct, the effort to breed it out by eugenical measures is, in the present state of our knowledge, not to be recommended and that more fruitful approaches to crime are to be found in social measures of one type or another."

As to mental disease, mental defect and feeble-mindedness, although these are distinct clinical entities, there is no agreement about their heritable quality among experts. Mendel's laws, despite modifications, are still the basis of the science of heredity. Mendel's first law, of dominance, showed that when two pure bred plants with contrasting characters are cross bred, all the offspring of this first mating will show only one of two characters. The character apparent in the offspring is dominant, that which is hidden, recessive. Mendel's second law laid down that the characters which appear in the original organism are transmitted to the offspring without being changed or lost. Thirdly, he established that a hidden recessive character in a hybrid offspring may reappear in a later generation.

Mendel posited that corresponding to every inherited character are certain determiners or genes. His early followers assumed that a defective mind corresponded with a single defective gene, but later research has shown that they greatly oversimplified the problem. There are in fact many different types of genes whose absence or combination may result in defect or disease. To eradicate mental defect it would be necessary to sterilize not only the defective but also all "carriers", who themselves exhibit no abnormality, but whose organism contains recessive genes, which will appear as a defect in later generations. Since carriers far outnumber defectives, the amount of disease and deficiency which can be eradicated by sterilization of the latter is extremely small.

The present state of knowledge of heredity in this context is summed up best in the words of Professor L. S. Penrose, whose book on the subject, *Outline of Human Genetics*, was published in 1959:

> A not uncommon view [states Professor Penrose] is that it should be possible, by sterilization or other such methods, to prevent the transmission of unfavourable genes and thus reduce the incidence of hereditary defects in the population. Emphasis on this aspect of eugenics is now much less popular than formerly for a variety of reasons, quite apart from the dangers of the misapplication of schemes from political motives. For example, it is now widely realized that the eugenic effects of any superficial sterilization scheme must be rather slight as compared with the effort required to enforce it. Recessive abnormalities are only very rarely propagated by affected parents; they appear among the children of normal carriers. Little effect can be produced by preventing homozygotes from breeding, since they very rarely breed anyway and, when they do, their children are quite likely to be normal. Attacking the disease by sterilizing all heterozygotes is theoretically possible but terribly wasteful. Indeed if, as is generally believed, every person is heterozygous for one or more recessive defects, the project is absurd. The more practical remedy, advocating that carriers of the same defect should be discouraged from mating with one another, would efficiently diminish occurrence of abnormal homozygotes and would be eugenically acceptable.[1]

Quite apart from the vexed question of heredity, the problem of eradicating mental disease and defect is made virtually insoluble by ignorance of the pathology of mental defect and many diseases, and the non-hereditary quality of

[1] See Chapter VI, p. 119 f.

others. Arterio-sclerosis and senile dementia, general paresis, and alcoholism display no hereditary factor. Schizophrenia and manic-depression are thought to be constitutional and hereditary by the majority, but their pathology is still subject to dispute and uncertainty. Epilepsy is thought to be hereditary, but this has not been established beyond all doubt. Mental defect and feeble-mindedness are probably caused by genetic factors, but since these are present in many "carriers" sterilization of defectives does not solve the problem. It has been estimated that 89 per cent of feeble-mindedness comes from parents who appear normal but are in fact carriers. "We assume", concludes the Brock report, "that the Legislature would not feel justified in compelling any persons to submit to sterilization, unless it could be shown beyond reasonable doubt that some at least of their offspring would either be mentally defective or would develop mental disorder. In the present state of knowledge no such proof can be produced." It could be argued that compulsory sterilization is justified on environmental rather than hereditary grounds, since it would prevent children from being brought up in unsuitable homes and by inadequate parents, but if this is to be the criterion, there is no logical reason for limiting it to mental defectives.

The Brock report came out against any programme of compulsory sterilization but did recommend that voluntary sterilization should be available to certain classes of people. It suggested first that those who are mentally defective or have suffered from mental disorder should be able to avail themselves of sterilization. A second category, it suggested, should be those who are suffering from, or who are believed to be carriers of grave physical disorders which have been shown to be transmissible. Finally, sterilization should be available to those who are believed to be likely to transmit mental disorder or defect. The authorization of the Ministry of Health would be necessary as well as the support of two medical practitioners. Doubtful cases would be referred to a small medical committee. The scheme seems simple enough in theory, but how, it may legitimately be asked, would it be possible to show that the consent given was in fact voluntary? Many defectives would be unable to grasp the significance of a sterilizing operation and any consent they might give would be purely notional. Opportunity would be opened for the exercising of undue influence and the possibility of abuse would be a real one.

What is the attitude of English law to sterilization? Compulsory sterilization would clearly be a criminal offence, but what of the voluntary variety? A sterilization performed on therapeutic grounds for the safeguarding of a patient's health would be legally permissible in the opinion of most lawyers, although there is no English case directly on the point. There are, however, two United States cases which are relevant. In 1934 the Supreme Court of Minnesota, in the case of *Christensen* v. *Thornby*, held that such an operation is not against public policy and that medical necessity constituted sufficient grounds for its performance. In 1952 in *Danielson* v. *Roche*, a Californian case, a doctor removed his patient's Fallopian tubes in the course of an operation when he discovered that they were infected. He was sued by the patient but judgement for the doctor was given and upheld on appeal.

Sterilization for eugenic or contraceptive purposes is of doubtful status at English law. The question turns in the first place as to whether sterilization is to be regarded as a maim. No one has a right at common law to consent to the infliction of bodily harm on himself which amounts to a maim, in the absence of just cause. Coke records a case at Leicester of 1604 where a "young strong and lustie rogue, to make himself impotent, thereby to have the more colour to begge or to be relieved without putting himself to any labour, caused his companion to strike off his left hand." Both were fined for committing a criminal offence. Is sterilization a maim? Castration has been held to be a maim but sterilization is not the same thing. It has been argued that sterilization is not a maim, since the essence of a maim was that it lessened a man's ability to fight. In his digest Stephen defines a maim as "bodily harm whereby a man is deprived of the use of any member of his body or of any sense which he can use in fighting, or by the loss of which he is generally and permanently weakened, but a bodily injury is not a maim merely because it is a disfigurement" (article 290). Furthermore, the law of maim did not apply to women and would not, it has been alleged, apply today. However, even if sterilization is admitted not to be a maim, the question is not disposed of since it might well be classified as an assault and battery, and here again consent without any justifying cause is no defence. In 1949 the three medical defence organizations obtained the opinion of counsel as to whether sterilization of men or women is a legal operation. They received the reply that sterilization on therapeutic grounds was legal but not if it was performed on eugenic grounds. Other counsel have advised that if the eugenic grounds are well founded the sterilization, provided of course consent had been obtained, would not be illegal.

The most important case on sterilization at English law is that of *Bravery* v. *Bravery*, a court of appeal case of 1954. The case concerned two parties who were married in 1934 and who had a child two years later in 1936. In 1938 the husband underwent sterilization but his wife continued to cohabit with him until she left him in 1951. The wife sued for a divorce on the ground of cruelty, but this was denied her by both the High Court and the Court of Appeal with Lord Justice Denning dissenting. The majority of the Court of Appeal found that on its facts the case did not establish cruelty but they did not hold that sterilization itself was legal since in their view it was not in issue. They did, however, state that "as between husband and wife for a man to submit himself to such a process without good medical reason ... would, no doubt, unless his wife were a consenting party, be a grave offence to her which could without difficulty be shown to be a cruel act, if it were found to have injured her health or to have caused reasonable apprehension of such injury. It is also not difficult to imagine that if a husband submitted to such an operation without the wife's consent, and if the latter desired to have children, the hurt would be progressive to the nerves and health of the wife." Lord Justice Denning in the course of his dissenting judgement went much further than his fellow judges, but since his remarks were not required by the facts of the case they must be regarded as *obiter dicta* and therefore of reduced authority.

Referring to sterilization, Lord Justice Denning said:

> When it is done with the man's consent for a just cause, it is quite lawful, as, for instance, when it is done to prevent the transmission of an hereditary disease; but when it is done without just cause or excuse, it is unlawful, even though the man consents to it. Take a case where a sterilization operation is done so as to enable a man to have the pleasure of sexual intercourse without the responsibilities attaching to it. The operation then is plainly injurious to the public interest. It is degrading to the man himself. It is injurious to his wife and to any women whom he may marry, to say nothing of the way it opens to licentiousness; and, unlike contraceptives, it allows no room for a change of mind on either side. It is illegal even though the man consents to it. . . . If a husband undergoes an operation for sterilization without just cause or excuse, he strikes at the very root of the marriage relationship. The divorce court should not countenance such an operation for sterilization any more than the criminal courts. It is severe cruelty.

Lord Justice Denning's view thus appears to be that while therapeutic and even eugenic sterilization may be lawful, sterilization for contraceptive purposes is not.

England has no sterilization statutes but they are found in twenty-eight of the American States. All of these statutes have a eugenic purpose and are intended to restrict the spread of insanity, mental deficiency, feeble-mindedness, etc. Normally they authorize vasectomy or salpingectomy as a means of carrying out sterilization. The Nebraska statute has an overtly punitive purpose and provides castration for male inmates of certain institutions who have been committed for rape, incest or crimes against nature. Twenty-three States provide for compulsory sterilization, two for voluntary and three for both types of procedure. In fourteen States the compulsory provisions are mandatory and in twelve permissive. The feeble-minded are included in all the statutes and the insane in the majority. Two-thirds of the statutes designate epileptics as subjects for sterilization and over a third, criminals. A quarter of the statutes mention moral degenerates and sexual perverts, and one State, Georgia, provides for sterilization of those suffering from physical disease. In most States special administrative boards make the decision to sterilize, although appeal to the courts is generally provided for.

Up to 1925 all sterilization statutes challenged in the courts were held unconstitutional, but in that year in both Michigan and Virginia, sterilization statutes were upheld by the courts. The Virginia case, that of *Buck* v. *Bell*, was taken to the Supreme Court of the United States where the statute was held to be constitutional. From then until 1942 judicial policy favoured sterilization statutes, but in that year the Supreme Court in *Skinner* v. *Oklahoma* held that the Oklahoma statute violated the equal protection clause of the fourteenth amendment to the Constitution. The case marked a reaction against sterilization as such and since its decision the validity of all the State sterilization statutes has been in doubt.

The constitutional issue is a complex one and the sterilization statutes can be challenged on a number of grounds. The most fundamental is whether sterilization for eugenic purposes violates the fundamental rights to life, liberty and the pursuit of happiness laid down in the Declaration of Independence. In *Buck* v. *Bell*, Justice Holmes made it clear that in his opinion it does not:

> We have seen [declared the judge] more than once that the public welfare may call upon its best citizens for their lives. It

would be strange if it could not call upon those who already sap the strength of the State for these lesser sacrifices, often not felt to be such by those concerned, in order to prevent our being swamped with incompetents. It is better for all the world, if instead of waiting to execute degenerate offspring for crime, or to let them starve for their imbecility, society can prevent those who are manifestly unfit from continuing their kind. The principle that sustains compulsory vaccination is broad enough to cover cutting the Fallopian tubes. Three generations of imbeciles are enough.

Another ground for challenging sterilization is that it violates the fourteenth amendment to the Constitution which provides that no State shall "deny to any person within its jurisdiction the equal protection of the laws". The amendment does not automatically forbid all statutes which apply to one class only, which may be held valid if the class has a reasonable and not an arbitrary basis, and the law applies alike to all persons similarly situated. In 1942 the Supreme Court in *Skinner* v. *Oklahoma* struck down the Oklahoma sterilization statute which authorized the compulsory sterilization of habitual criminals, who had been convicted of "felonies involving moral turpitude". "When the law lays an unequal hand on those who have committed intrinsically the same quality of offence," said Justice Douglas, "and sterilizes one and not the other, it has made as invidious a discrimination as if it had selected a particular race or nationality for oppressive treatment."

The fourteenth amendment also provides that no State shall deprive any person of life, liberty or property "without due process of law". This means that any citizen threatened by statute with deprivation of rights must be given notice of this intention and an opportunity to be heard. Several of the sterilization statutes in the United States have been declared invalid on this ground but others have been upheld. It would seem that the minimum requirements for compliance with this provision of the fourteenth amendment are hearing on reasonable notice before a duly constituted tribunal where the person to be sterilized has a right to appear. If the tribunal is not itself a court, then a right to appeal to a court for review must be included.

By the eighth amendment to the American Constitution any "cruel and unusual punishment" is forbidden, and sterilization statutes have been challenged as contravening this provision. The courts have reached conflicting decisions, the Iowa and Nevada courts, for example, having struck down statutes which provided sterilization as a punishment for criminals, but such a statute has been upheld in Washington. The sterilization of mental defectives has been consistently held to be non-punitive. "The only purpose of this constitutional provision", said the judge in *Smith* v. *Command*, a Michigan case of 1925, "is to place a limitation on the power of the legislature in fixing punishment for crime. There is no element of punishment involved in the sterilization of feeble-minded persons. In this respect it is analogous to compulsory vaccination. Both are non-punitive. It is therefore plainly apparent that the constitutional inhibition against cruel or unusual punishment has no application to the surgical treatment of feeble-minded persons. It has reference only to punishment after convictions of crimes."

Judicial attitudes in the United States to sterilization statutes have undergone a change since the high-water mark of approval was reached in *Buck* v. *Bell*. A second case came before the Supreme Court, as has been noted, in 1942, *Skinner* v. *Oklahoma*. The judgement of the court was distinctly unfavourable to sterilization:

This case touches a sensitive and important area of human rights. Oklahoma deprives certain individuals of a right which is basic to the perpetuation of a race—the right to have offspring. . . . The power to sterilize if exercised may have subtle, far-reaching and devastating effects. In evil or reckless hands it can cause races or types which are inimical to the dominant group to wither and disappear. There is no redemption for the individual whom it touches. Any experiment which the State conducts is to his irreparable injury. He is for ever deprived of a basic liberty. . . . Strict scrutiny of the classification which a state makes in a sterilization law is essential, lest unwittingly or otherwise, invidious discriminations are made against groups or types of individuals in violation of the constitutional guaranty of just and equal laws [Justice Douglas].

Judicial disapproval of sterilization has been matched by a decline in the number of sterilizations actually carried out. The total number of sterilizations effected in the United States between 1907, the date of the first sterilization law, and 1958 was 60,166, of which 24,008 were male and 36,158 female. In the past fifteen years the number of sterilizations carried out has steadily decreased. For the five-year period 1941–6, 9,200 sterilizations were reported: in the next five-year period this had dropped to 7,100, and for the five years 1951–6 it had fallen to 6,100. Some States have had their statutes declared unconstitutional: others while retaining them on the statute book have made no use of them. It seems likely that a further decline in the number of sterilizations will take place in the future.

The Catholic Church condemns all forms of direct sterilization, whether compulsory or voluntary. Her condemnation is based on traditional Christian ethics which lays great emphasis on the essential creatureliness of man. Man is not the absolute master of his own body, but holds it on trust for God's purposes. His procreative faculty is one of man's most important endowments and save in cases of grave necessity he is not free to do away with it at will. Sterilization involves not only a mutilation of the body but the deprivation of a major faculty. In the early Church some persons, misunderstanding the meaning of Matthew 19.12 ("there be eunuchs who have made themselves eunuchs for the kingdom of heaven's sake"), castrated themselves. Such practices were condemned both by canon law and the Fathers of the Church. Castration, they taught, for the spiritual end of preserving chastity is ineffectual, and in any case is wrong because it is a kind of suicide, and implies that the body which God has created is in itself evil. Implicitly it denies free will and the providence of God.

In the Middle Ages St Thomas developed Catholic teaching holding that a man who mutilates his body commits a threefold offence: against the natural law of self-preservation and proper self-love; against the community of which he is a part; and also against God. To mutilate the body in order to preserve chastity is disproportionate. St Thomas allowed one exception to his rule, the removal of a diseased part of the body for the good of the whole. "If, however," he writes in the *Summa Theologica*,[2] "the member be decayed and therefore a source of corruption to the whole body, then it is lawful with the consent of the owner of the member, to cut away the member for the welfare of the whole body, since each one is entrusted with the care of his own welfare. The same applies if it be done with the consent of the person whose business it is to care for the welfare of the person who has a decayed member; otherwise it is altogether unlawful to maim anyone." In his Encyclical *Casti Connubii*, Pius XI confirmed the teaching of St Thomas. "Christian teaching established," he wrote, "and the light of human reason makes it most clear, that private individuals have no other power over the members of their bodies than that which pertains to their natural ends; and they are not free to destroy or mutilate their members, or in any other way render themselves unfit for their natural functions, except when no other provision can be made for the good of the whole body."

What is the Catholic and Christian attitude to sterilization carried out by the State? St Thomas concludes that since the State has the right to punish criminals by death, it therefore has the right to impose the lesser penalty of mutilation. Whatever the logic of this argument it would not appeal greatly to Christians today who would be prevented by humanitarian

[2] IIa–IIae, art. 65.

reasons from putting it into effect. Moralists would be equally united in condemning the papal practice of castrating singing boys of the Sistine choir in order to preserve their treble voices, which was at one time tolerated.

Is a compulsory sterilization policy by the State justified on eugenic grounds? Some Catholic writers have attempted to justify sterilization of this kind on grounds of necessity in order to protect society from inundation by criminals and defectives. As has been already demonstrated this argument has an insecure factual basis and in any case segregation is always possible as an alternative. The approach of these writers must also be rejected on grounds of principle. Mental and physical defects are misfortunes, not crimes or sins, and public authority, in the words of Pius XII, has no right to have sterilization carried out "to the harm of the innocent". The compulsory sterilization argument is based on the assumption that only the strong and the fit have a right to live unmaimed, and it is only a short step from this to the conclusion that they have no right to life at all. State policies of compulsory sterilization must therefore be rejected without qualification.

What of voluntary sterilization? Catholic theologians recognize that therapeutic sterilization is morally justified if it is the only means of securing the welfare of the body as a whole. Its employment would fall within the Thomist exception already mentioned. Sterilization in circumstances where a woman's health would be gravely endangered by a further pregnancy would not, however, be justified, since there is always the alternative of refraining from sexual intercourse. The purpose of such sterilization is simply contraceptive. Indirect sterilization is also permissible, such as the performance of an operation to remove a woman's diseased womb, where the intention is to save her life and the sterilization is an incidental effect. This is an example of applying the moral theological principle of double effect, which states that an action not in itself intrinsically evil, followed by both a good and a bad result, may be performed provided that the good and not the evil effect is directly intended, that the good effect is not produced by means of the evil effect, and a grave reason exists for allowing the evil to occur. Voluntary sterilization for eugenic reasons is not countenanced by the Church.

It is clear that a State policy of compulsory sterilization is contrary to Christian moral principles, since it is an invasion of the rights of the human person and gives to the State powers to which it has no claim. The benefits which are said to result from such a policy are, as has been seen, so indefinite that even on non-moral grounds such a sterilization policy cannot be justified. Christians are thus under a duty to oppose the introduction of any such schemes and to work for the repeal of laws which authorize them. Should voluntary sterilization be permitted by law? Applying Christian ethics there is no case for the legalizing of voluntary sterilization for contraceptive purposes. Such sterilization directly injures the common good by depriving the community of potentially healthy stock. By removing fear of pregnancy it might also encourage immorality and lead to the spread of venereal disease. Voluntary sterilization for eugenic purposes is a somewhat different matter. Pius XI has stated that public authority has no right to permit sterilization "under the pretext of any *indication* whatsoever", but a case can be made out for a law allowing voluntary sterilization for eugenic purposes. If those who have good reason to think that they will transmit disease or mental defect are permitted to sterilize themselves, it is difficult to see how the common good suffers. The decision is left to individuals to take themselves, following the light of their own conscience, and the State in no way approves of such a course. It can of course be argued that the introduction of legalized sterilization even in this limited form would lead to a demand for its extension and that on this ground it should be opposed.

A final word may be said on the position of Catholics in the medical and legal professions. Catholic doctors and nurses would be prevented by their ethical code from taking part in any sterilization operation save those of a strictly therapeutic kind. Catholic judges are bound to apply the law as it stands, but they are also bound by their conscience not to oblige anyone to commit an intrinsically immoral act. A compulsory sterilization order would undoubtedly fall within this category. Faced with this situation a Catholic judge would be obliged either to arrange not to hear the case or, in the last resort if this proves impossible, to resign his office.

CHAPTER VII

HOMOSEXUALITY

The Catholic Church and indeed Christians in general have always condemned homosexual activities as gravely sinful. This is not, of course, to state that the fact of homosexual orientation is in itself sinful. It is only when the disposition finds expression in external actions that the censure of the Church is incurred. This condemnation of homosexuality goes back to the Jewish period when any form of homosexual conduct was rejected as being contrary to the law of God. Undoubtedly the Lot story in *Genesis* played a major part in forming the Jewish attitude (Gen. 19. 4–8). It will be recalled that two angels were sent by God to investigate the situation in Sodom and, according to the traditional interpretation, the men of Sodom demanded to have intercourse with them. Lot, whose guests they were, resisted the demand, and the city was eventually destroyed for this attempted sacrilege and its general wickedness.

In the biblical passage the men of Sodom demand to "know" the angels, and this has been interpreted to mean a desire to have sexual intercourse with them, an interpretation supported by Lot's offer to the citizens of his daughters. It seems as though he is offering a heterosexual experience with them in order to distract their interest from his guests. This view of the Lot story depends on the acceptance of the word "know" as meaning know in the coital sense, but this has recently been challenged. In the *Encyclopaedia of Religion and Ethics*, Dr G. A. Barton has put forward the view that "know" has no sexual significance but merely means to get acquainted with. He has been supported by the Anglican scholar, Dr S. Bailey, in his book *Homosexuality and the Western Christian Tradition*. Dr Bailey agrees with Dr Barton in his interpretation of the word "know", and adds the further argument that none of the passages in the Bible which refer to homosexuality make any reference to Sodom. In Dr Bailey's view the offer of Lot's daughters is made to appease the crowds suspicious of the angels who might have designs against the city. He argues that the homosexual interpretation of the Lot story is not found until the second century B.C. and represents the reaction of the Jewish people against the prevalence of homosexual practices in the pagan world. The importance of Dr Bailey's interpretation is that if accepted it means that homosexual sins have not been singled out for special punishment by God, and the Christian moralist is free to evaluate them, applying the ordinary principles of moral philosophy and theology, leaving this part of revelation out of consideration.

Whatever one's view of the Sodom story the condemnation of homosexuality in the Old Testament is clear. "Thou shalt not lie with mankind, as with womankind", says Leviticus; "it is abomination" (19. 22). The punishment for this is laid down as death by stoning. There is, however, no evidence that this penalty was enforced. No doubt exists that the Jewish people rejected homosexuality with abhorrence, but it must be seen in the perspective of their rejection of other sexual sins. Jewish writers were equally forthright in their condemnation of adultery and fornication and said so much more frequently.

St Paul in the New Testament echoes the Jewish condemnation of homosexual practice in a well-known passage. He denounces the idolatry of the Gentiles and adds: "That is why God abandoned their lustful hearts to filthy practices of dishonouring their own bodies among themselves. They had exchanged God's truth for a lie, reverencing and worshipping

the creature in preference to the Creator (blessed is he for
ever, Amen); and, in return, God abandoned them to passions
which brought dishonour to themselves. Their women exchanged natural for unnatural intercourse; and the men, on
their side, giving up natural intercourse with women, were
burnt up with desire for each other; men practising vileness
with their fellow men. Thus they have received a fitting
retribution for their false belief" (Rom. 1. 24–8). Here St Paul
implies that the descent to homosexual practices was in some
way a punishment for indulging in idolatry, but the connection between the two seems obscure. The Church Fathers were
forthright in their denunciation of homosexual sins, pre-
sumably because of the prevalence of homosexuality in the
contemporary Roman world. The sins against nature, declared
St Augustine in his *Confessions*, "like those of the men of
Sodom, are in all times and places to be detested and
punished. Even if all nations committed such sins, they
should all alike be held guilty of God's law which did not
make men so that they should use each other thus. The friendship which should be between God and us is violated when
nature—whose author he is—is polluted by so perverted a
lust."

Under the Republic laws had existed punishing homosexual
conduct, but they were not enforced in the pagan empire.
When the empire became Christian new enactments were
passed. In 390, Valentinian ordered that sodomists should be
burned, but it is doubtful whether the penalty was enforced.
Justinian issued two *novellae* on homosexuality, but they laid
more stress on repentance than on punishment. They are
interesting in illustrating a long-lived superstition that all
kinds of disaster, including famine, pestilence and earth-
quakes, result from homosexual conduct. Ecclesiastical law
also penalized homosexual practices but with spiritual
penalties. Accordingly the Council of Elvira, held in Southern
Spain (305–6), forbade communion to be given to *stupratores
puerorum.*

In medieval times polemicists, such as Peter Damian, in-
veighed against homosexuality, but their diatribes were of less
influence than St Thomas Aquinas's temperate treatment of
the subject in his *Summa Theologica*. St Thomas wrote that
homosexual sins were contrary to "right reason" and "contrary to the natural order of the venereal act as becoming to
the human race". Since the purpose of the sexual act is procreation its end is directly frustrated by homosexual practices.
St Thomas gave a philosophical form to the teachings of St Paul
and his writing was of great influence. Ecclesiastical law continued to punish homosexual offences but the penalties were
spiritual. Dr Kinsey's wild assertion that the medieval period
provides "abundant records" of the imposition of the death
penalty is not supported by any evidence.

English law dealt with homosexual offences from early
times. According to *Fleta*, a legal treatise of the year 1290,
the horrible penalty of burying alive was prescribed for
sodomy. Later another legal treatise laid down burning as the
right punishment. It is highly unlikely that these penalties
were enforced, and in fact homosexual conduct was dealt with
by more merciful penalties in the ecclesiastical courts. When
Henry VIII transferred jurisdiction from these courts to the
common law courts in a statute of 1533, a preamble to the
statute declared that there was not yet "sufficient and condign
punishment" for these abominable offences. The statute laid
down the death penalty for sodomy, and it was spasmodically
enforced during the next three hundred years. In 1631, for
example, the Earl of Castlehaven was executed for the rape of
his wife and sodomy with his servants. Coke and Blackstone
were outspoken in their condemnation of homosexuality. In
his *Institutes* Coke denounced it as a "detestable and abominable sin, among Christians not to be named". Blackstone was
no less censorious: "This the voice of nature and of reason,
and the express law of God determine to be capital. Of which
we have a signal instance long before the Jewish dispensation,

by the destruction of two cities by fire from heaven; so that this is an universal, not merely a provincial precept."

No change was made in English law until the nineteenth century. In 1861 Victorian humanitarians secured the abolition of the death penalty for sodomy and a term of penal servitude from ten years to life was substituted. In 1885 the Criminal Law Amendment Act provided that any male person, guilty of committing or procuring, or attempting to procure, an act of gross indecency with another male "in public or private", should be guilty of a misdemeanour, punishable with a maximum term of two years' imprisonment, with or without hard labour. In its original form the Bill made no mention of homosexual offences, and the clause was introduced early in the morning by Henry Labouchere and added to the Bill without discussion. Since 1885 the law has remained virtually unchanged. In 1954 a special departmental committee, under the chairmanship of Sir John Wolfenden, was appointed to consider the problem of homosexual offences and published its report in 1957. The committee recommended that private homosexual acts between consenting adults should no longer be criminal offences. Three years later the Commons discussed the report but a motion calling on the government to implement the report was defeated by 213 votes to 99. In 1956 the law dealing with sexual offences was consolidated in a single statute but it made no substantive alteration in the law.

United States law on homosexual offences was greatly influenced by English law, and homosexual acts between males are punished in all the States. The type of acts punished, however, and the punishment laid down, varies from State to State. Penalties may be as low as one year's imprisonment with a maximum of three, as in Virginia; or as high as a minimum of seven years, as in Rhode Island; or a maximum of sixty years, as in North Carolina. Some States distinguish between different types of offences, and penalties are graded according to which offence is committed and whether there are aggravating circumstances. No comprehensive figures are available on law enforcement but in some States certainly the law appears to be only spasmodically enforced. In New York City, for example, in 1948 there were only 146 arrests for sodomy and in 1949 the figure was 112. From 1950–4 only eighty-nine sodomy cases were reported in the United States of which twenty-seven were in California, nine in Texas and five in New York. Nearly all the cases involved some public element. In England figures for prosecutions and convictions have been made available through the Wolfenden report, which show that the English laws are not dead letters. Indictable cases rose from 390 in 1931 to 2,504 in 1955. For the three years ending in March 1956, 300 adult offenders were convicted for offences committed in private with consenting adults. Homosexual conduct between women is not punished in England, and although it may be theoretically in America, it is so rare as to be negligible in practice.

The Catholic and traditional Christian attitude to homosexuality was developed at a time when there was little knowledge of either the extent or causes of homosexuality, and today these approaches need to be modified in the light of new knowledge. Homosexuality is now known to be much more widespread than was thought in the past, as the researches of Dr Kinsey and others have shown. In the first of the Kinsey reports, published in 1948, on the American male, Dr Kinsey used case histories of 12,000 men. He concluded that 37 per cent of the male population of the United States had had some homosexual experience between the beginning of adolescence and old age. For males who had remained single until the age of thirty-five, the figure rose to 50 per cent. Of the male population 25 per cent had more than incidental homosexual experience or reactions for at least three years between the ages of sixteen and fifty-five. Of the males 8 per cent were exclusively homosexual for at least three years within these age limits, and 4 per cent of the white males were exclusively homosexual throughout their lives after the onset of adolescence. Dr Kinsey and his assistants found these results startling, but when they were checked they yielded the same result. An aberration is not, of course, right, because it exists, as Kinsey at times assumes, but the figures do indicate that homosexuality is not a problem confined to a tiny group of perverts but one of much wider social significance.

What are the causes of homosexuality? Medical evidence and opinion can supply no agreed answer, but it is widely accepted that apart from perverts who have turned to homosexual practices entirely of their own free will, there are inverts, who form the majority, whose psycho-sexual impulses are directed more or less exclusively towards persons of the same sex. Traditional Christian thought has been ignorant of this state of inversion and has tended to regard the whole problem as one of perversion without extenuating circumstances. The Augustinian-Thomist approach needs to be modified in the light of present medical knowledge with less stress laid on the unnatural character of such acts since, as far as the invert is concerned, homosexual practice is more in accord with his own subjective nature than heterosexual activity.

Some doctors regard homosexuality as a congenital anomaly.

> All grades are found [states the Catholic report to the Wolfenden Committee] from physical pseudo-hermaphroditism down to apparent physical and temperamental normality. The origin of this condition is not always clear, although there is much to suggest that it depends primarily on a lack of balance between the various glands of internal secretion. Apart from the misdirection of sexual impulse, inverts may be perfectly normal in every other respect although it is true that moral and social conflicts arising equally from the frustration of their sexual lives and the gratification of their—to them perfectly normal—impulses frequently lead to neurosis, but such neurosis is adventitious rather than part and parcel of their condition.

Others regard homosexuality not as a physical manifestation but as psycho-genetically acquired misdirection of the sexual impulse. Opinions vary widely as to the cause of this misdirection. Thus Freudians maintain that all humans are potentially bisexual and pass consciously or unconsciously through a homosexual phase. Sexual inverts fail to make the transition because they have not successfully resolved the Oedipus complex. Adlerians think homosexuality is caused by an inferiority complex owing to which homosexual males doubt their ability to dominate the opposite sex. Others think that homosexuality springs from a traumatic experience suffered in early years.

As medical knowledge of the state and causes of inversion has grown so have suggestions for the alteration of the laws which punish homosexuals. On both sides of the Atlantic authoritative committees, the Wolfenden Committee in England, a committee of and the Council of the American Law Institute in the U.S.A., have suggested that homosexual acts which take place in private between consenting adults should no longer be subject to the criminal law. This is already the case in the majority of European States. On the continent of Europe only Austria and Germany punish such offences.

Does Catholic moral thought require the maintenance of a legal ban on all forms of homosexual behaviour or would it favour the sort of change proposed by the Wolfenden Committee? Some guidance on this problem is given in the report of the Committee appointed by the late Cardinal Griffin to advise the Wolfenden Committee on Catholic views, whose report was published in the *Dublin Review* in 1956. The Committee concluded that existing English law does not effectively distinguish between sin, which is a matter of private morals, and crime, which is an offence against the State having anti-social consequences. It concluded that the law was inequitable in its incidence and that its punishments were imposed on a small minority of offenders and often on those who least deserved to be imprisoned. The Committee recommended that the criminal law should be amended so as to exclude consensual acts done in private by adult males but that penal sanctions should be maintained to restrain offences against minors, offences against public decency and the exploitation of vice for the purpose of gain. The Committee reached the conclusion that imprisonment is largely ineffectual to re-orientate those with homosexual tendencies and usually has deleterious effects on them, while at the same time rejecting as unsatisfactory the suggestion that institutions should be set up exclusively for homosexuals.

A further argument for changing the law is that it is a fertile source of blackmail. The Wolfenden Committee gave some figures for 1950, when thirty-two of the seventy-one cases reported to the police for blackmail were connected with homosexual offences. Some years earlier, speaking in the House of Lords, Lord Jowitt, a former Lord Chancellor, disclosed that when he was Attorney-General, 95 per cent of the blackmail cases coming to his attention arose from homosexuality. In the United States the law has also lent itself to blackmail. Judge Ploscowe, in his book *Sex and the Law*, reported that in 1940 the New York District Attorney broke up a blackmailing ring that had been operating for twenty years in and around New York City. Twenty-three members of the ring were sent to prison.

If homosexuals in general are not to be sent to prison in the absence of aggravating circumstances, how are they to be treated? Suggestions have been made that they should be subject to castration, a course indignantly rejected by the Catholic Committee. They added, however, that they accepted "the propriety of the use for good cause under medical supervision of drugs to suppress sexual desire and activity, with the consent of the patient. Such treatment is permissible where serious pathological conditions obtain and when other remedies have proved ineffectual." Other methods that are open to the courts are absolute or conditional discharge, binding over, fining or placing on probation. Probation probably offers the best method of dealing with homosexual cases where there has been no duress or violence, and the courts may on medical evidence make the reception of medical treatment a condition of probation. Grave obstacles to the successful treatment of homosexual offenders are the shortage of psychiatrists and ignorance of the etiology of homosexuality. The Wolfenden Committee could find little evidence of homosexuals having been re-orientated to heterosexuality. Treatment may, however, be directed towards securing a better adaptation to life and the strengthening of powers of self-control. Clearly a crying need is for further research into the whole subject.

In helping the homosexual adapt himself to society, or in rehabilitating him after he has been to prison or come before the courts, the Church has an important part to play. Priests need to be equipped with a certain amount of psychiatric knowledge and they must also have understanding and sympathy if they are to help the homosexual effectively. As the Church of England report *Pastor and Homosexual* points out, there is always some hope for the heterosexual who desires marriage but for the homosexual there is none. "It is one thing", says the report, "to grow reconciled to the fact that the chance of marriage is gradually receding, or to accept chastity in response to a vocation which may perhaps be fortified by vows of celibacy; it is another to know from the outset that one's condition excludes the legitimate satisfaction of sexual desires which are nonetheless clamant for being disorientated. No good is done by pretending that the invert's position is other than it really is: it is a tragic situation and he must be aided and encouraged to face it with the heroism it demands."

Until recently there was very little written on homosexuality from the pastoral point of view and much of this was inaccurate or positively misleading. The situation is fortunately now improving and books such as Fr George Hagmaier's

Moral Problems Now and articles such as Fr Harvey's "Homosexuality as a Pastoral Problem", published in *Theological Studies* (March 1955), are helpful. Much more needs to be written from the spiritual and medical point of view if priests are to discharge their duties adequately in this difficult field.

SELECT BIBLIOGRAPHY

In this series: DOMINIAN, J.: *Psychiatry and the Christian*;
FABRÈGUES, Jean de: *Christian Marriage*; MARSHALL, John:
Medicine and Morals; SORAS, Alfred de, S.J.: *International
Morality*; TREVETT, R. F.: *The Church and Sex* (English
edn, *Sex and the Christian*).

BUCKLEY, M. J.: *Morality and the Homosexual*, Westminster,
Md, Newman Press, 1960.

DAWSON, C.: *Religion and the Modern State*, London and New
York, Sheed and Ward, 1938.

FLETCHER, Joseph: *Morals and Medicine*, Princeton, N.J., Princeton Univ. Press, 1954.

FORD, J. C., and KELLY, G.: *Contemporary Moral Theology*,
Westminster, Md, Newman Press, and Cork, Mercier Press.
1958.

GLEASON, R., and HAGMAIER, G.: *Counselling the Catholic*, London and New York, Sheed and Ward, 1959.

HALLOWELL, J. H.: *Moral Foundation of Democracy*, Chicago,
University of Chicago Press, 1954.

HART, H. L. A.: *Law, Liberty and Morality*, London and New
York, Oxford Univ. Press, 1963.

HEALY, E. F.: *Medical Ethics*, Chicago, Loyola Univ. Press, 1958.

KELLY, G.: *Medico-Moral Problems*, Dublin, Clonmore and
Reynolds, and Westminster, Md, Newman Press, 1955.

LESTAPIS, S. de, S.J.: *Family Planning and Modern Problems*,
London, Burns and Oates, and New York, Herder, 1961.

MARITAIN, J.: *The Person and the Common Good*, New York,
Scribners, 1947.

O'SULLIVAN, R. (editor): *Under God and the Law*, Westminster,
Md, Newman Press, 1949; *Inheritance of Common Law*,
Westminster, Md, Newman Press, 1951, and London, Oxford
Univ. Press, 1950.

PIEPER, J.: *Justice*, New York, Pantheon, 1955, and London,
Faber, 1957.

ST JOHN-STEVAS, N.: *Life, Death and the Law*, London, Eyre and
Spottiswoode, and Bloomington, Ind., Indiana Univ. Press,
1961.

The Twentieth Century
Encyclopedia of Catholicism

*The number of each volume indicates
its place in the over-all series
and not the order of publication.*

Titles are subject to change.